ASPECTS OF SOCIAL POLICY

Efficiency in the Social Services

Alan Williams &
Robert Anderson

D1608237

Efficiency in the Social Services

Aspects of Social Policy
General Editor: J. P. Martin
Professor of Sociology and Social Administration,
University of Southampton

Efficiency in
the Social Services

Alan Williams & Robert Anderson

BASIL BLACKWELL · OXFORD
MARTIN ROBERTSON · LONDON

ISBN 0 631 16570 3 (hardback)
       0 631 16580 0 (paperback)

First published in 1975
by Basil Blackwell & Mott Ltd, Oxford
and Martin Robertson and Co. Ltd, London

Set in Linotype Times
Printed in Great Britain by
Western Printing Services Ltd, Bristol
and bound at
The Kemp Hall Bindery, Oxford

Contents

Introduction

This book is intended to help the large number of people in the social services with responsibility for decisions (large and small) which commit resources that are in short supply, be these money, materials or manpower. Not many such decision makers or policy makers will have had any formal training in economics, though they will, by experience, by intuition, or by self-education, have picked up a great deal of the basic insights of that subject. Our experience in discussing policy issues with them* over the past five years or so, however, has led us to observe two grave weaknesses in the present situation. The first of these is that there is a danger that a casual and superficial acquaintance with the terminology of economics can often unwittingly deceive all parties into thinking that a systematic and fundamental understanding of its principles has been achieved. Secondly, those practitioners who are only too keenly aware of their own deficiencies in this field, and anxious to make them good, are daunted by the abstractness and apparent irrelevance of the typical textbook approach to the subject, and particularly with the central role played by profit-seeking behaviour, and the strong commercial overtones which consequently pervade the exposition.

In writing this book we have tried to remedy this situation by demonstrating that basic micro-economic principles are just as relevant in the non-commercial environment in which social services characteristically operate as they are in the field of business. All that needs to be presupposed is that people do not want to waste scarce resources, and that they have some ordering of priorities among the various good things which they are trying to achieve. Anyone in the social services who could identify himself or herself

* Especially in connection with the SSRC-financed Public Sector Studies Programme at the Institute of Social and Economic Research in the University of York, out of which the ideas for this book emerged.

with that presupposition should find something in this book relevant to his or her problems.

We have tried in the opening chapters to work from concrete situations, posing a simple down-to-earth problem, offering a solution (or a variety of solutions) then eliciting the principles which implicitly informed them. In the later chapters we have surveyed the kind of policy analysis which has been done, using these micro-economic principles, in particular fields in which we happen to have worked.* It would be quite possible to replicate these surveys for other fields such as education and housing not covered here. Because we have written with a mature and experienced adult readership in mind, we have not thought it necessary to catalogue all the possible applications of the ideas and concepts we have expounded. We have assumed that each reader will bring to bear, and draw upon, his or her own experiences, and since only the more alert and intellectually curious are ever likely to read a book such as this, we have relied on that alertness and curiosity to supply the imaginative leaps that enable people to recognize their problems as the same in substance as somebody else's, even though the setting and terminology may be different.

On the other hand, we hope that our readers will not feel insulted by our assumption that they come to this book with no knowledge of economics whatever, and that they are prepared to be led initially through apparently simple problems (which are later made more complex) in the interests of orderly exposition, and that they will not be disappointed at the end if what they finish up with is a changed perception of the way their problems can be formulated for solution, rather than a set of ready made answers to oversimplified questions.

We do not expect people, after having mastered the contents of this book, necessarily to be able to set up in business as efficiency experts in the social services. It is certainly not our intention to equip people for that rather specialized role. What we would hope for is that they will be able to see, very much more clearly than at present, where economic analysis could be helpful, how to use economics (and economists) intelligently without entertaining exaggerated or misplaced ideas about the extent to which clarification of problems leads to their solution, and, last but not least, to protect practitioners from being baffled by science when they find them-

---

* For the benefit of those readers who would like to tackle the more orthodox exposition of these same ideas in the standard textbooks, we have given some guide to further reading at the end of each chapter.

selves at the receiving end of complex pieces of policy analysis which purport to bear on the efficiency of social services. This we aim to do by providing a framework of thought which will generate intelligently critical and probing questions which should reveal the quality of the analytical work underlying any set of conclusions or recommendations.

We have not attempted to define the scope of the 'social services' at all closely, partly because the conventional institutional designations change from time to time, and differ markedly from one country to another, and what we have to say is not specific to any one country or any particular organizational structure. The essential test of relevance is the one mentioned earlier: is it a service with priorities and desire to conserve scarce resources, and is it attempting to do so without applying normal commercial criteria of financial profitability? If so, it fits *our* preconception of what a social service is, and what we have to say is potentially relevant to it.

Thus medical services may or may not be social services, education services may or may not be social services, housing may or may not be a social service, depending on whether or not they are operated in the manner stated. In some situations each may be wholly a social service, in others wholly a 'private' service (i.e. provided on strict commercial principles), and in yet others (and more commonly) each will operate on a 'mixed' basis (e.g. 'private' medicine/education/housing and 'socialized' medicine/education/housing may coexist), and a community which adopts one stance in one service may adopt quite a different one in another. We are not concerned here to recommend what an appropriate stance should be on any of these issues. We start from the fact that some 'social' (i.e. non-commercial) stance has been adopted, and proceed from there to explore what meaning can *then* be given to the notion of efficiency, and how it might be implemented.

If we have succeeded, even in this limited (though still very ambitious) task, we shall be only too pleased!

CHAPTER ONE

Preamble

1.1 The term 'efficiency'

1.11 'Efficiency' is a term with unfortunate connotations. Although it appears to some to be self-evidently a good thing, like 'sincerity' or 'honesty', just as with the pursuit of these latter virtues, there can be unattractive consequences. People do not like 'honesty' to be carried to the extreme where you *always* speak your mind, fully and without reserve, for the truth can often be hurtful, and there are circumstances in which inflicting such hurt is both unnecessary and unproductive of good. So it is with 'efficiency'; people do not like it carried to the extreme where it dominates all other considerations, and especially so in the social services, where the main purposes are the humane and just treatment of people, and often of people who are having rather a hard time anyway.

1.12 But to say that 'efficiency' is not the overriding consideration in the social services is not to imply that 'efficiency' is irrelevant. It would be extremely foolish not to adopt a new way of doing things which looked likely to perform at least as well as the old way and was at the same time less costly. Being 'less costly' means setting free scarce resources which can be used to provide other good things. In such a context everyone should favour efficiency quite unreservedly. The hesitations occur when notions of efficiency are applied which do not have these built-in safeguards about 'performance' being at least equally good.

1.13 Thus the antipathy to 'efficiency' stems from the much narrower interpretations of that term which are, unfortunately, rife. In particular, there is a brand of 'efficiency-mongering' which is obsessed with saving money (as if that were the only scarce resource) irrespective of the effects on performance. It has to be admitted, however, that at the other extreme stand equally blinkered people who think only in terms of performance and pay no regard to cost. If 'efficiency' is to be properly understood, and 'efficiency analysis' to be useful, then both 'costs' and 'effectiveness' need to be correctly interpreted and brought together in comprehensive, and comprehensible, systems of thought.

1.14 The object of this book is to do precisely that, namely, to show what are appropriate and inappropriate notions of cost and of effectiveness in particular contexts. We will try to show the limits of applicability of orthodox notions of 'efficiency' taken over from the world of business, but without rejecting them out-of-hand for, with careful reformulation and reinterpretation, there is much to be learned from that source.

1.15 We shall argue that it is not necessary to be 'hard-headed' in a commercial sense towards social services in order to be able to say relevant and useful things about their efficiency. But it *is* necessary to be 'hard thinking' in a humanitarian sense, assuming the objectives of services, how we know they are being fulfilled, and what weight we give to one objective compared with another when the necessity for choice arises.

1.16 There will be some who will deny the need for choice, and take refuge in slogans like 'nothing but the best is good enough, for . . .', or 'social needs . . .', or 'we must abolish . . .'. These may be useful catchphrases with which to intoxicate a befuddled audience in the course of a heated political debate, and may even form part of the carefully chosen armoury of pressure groups engaged in special pleading for sectional interests, but however deserving the objectives, notions of this kind do not constitute an adequate basis for a rational discourse about the level or pattern of social services in a democratic country, because they suppress vital information about what will be sacrificed if they are successful, and in a society which is short both of material resources and of human skills you can be sure that something will have to give if new tasks are accepted. Hence the necessity for choice.

1.17 The necessity for choice in the social services presents itself in a great variety of contexts. At one extreme lie the grand strategic issues concerning the balance between public services and private consumption, between universality and selectivity, between us and posterity, between health, education, housing, social security, and so on. At a much more mundane level there are matters such as whether old Mrs. X should have a home help, whether young Y should be entitled to (free) higher education, whether the Z family should be given priority on a council housing list because Mr. Z has deserted them. Each of these low level decisions implies the exercise of choice by someone, and consequently some assignment of priority by that person. The assignment of 'treatments' entails an assessment of the likely 'effectiveness' of the treatment, of the value of those expected effects, and hence an implicit judgement that the consequent costs borne by society (as a result of that decision) are worth incurring for the good so achieved. Each actor plays a part (however small) in shaping social policy, because everyone faces the problem of choice in allocating the resources at his command, even if they only be his own time and energy.

1.18 There is no dearth of books on social policy which purport to straighten us all out on the 'grand strategic issues'. Such books are frequently personal credo's or political manifesto's thinly disguised as sociological or economic analyses. Our intention is rather different. We do not aim to advise on *what policy should be* in any particular field, but on *how policy might be analysed and appraised.* We shall also operate at a very mundane level, well below that of social service policy makers as ordinarily understood, for the vast majority of the choices/decisions made in the social services are made by practitioners in the field, and it is to them, and to their immediate superiors, that this text is directed.

1.2 Some conventional reactions rejected

1.21 It is common to tackle the problem of efficiency by setting a norm (which purports to be an efficiency target) and then comparing individual performance with it. To be an acceptable procedure this requires that the norm itself be appropriately formulated, and that it is possible to check whether the circumstances in which the norm was derived (and for which it is relevant) are essentially similar to the circumstances in which it is being applied. These conditions are not always fulfilled.

1.22 The crudest kind of norm-based argument about efficiency runs like this: agency X spends 60 per cent of its budget on social workers, while we spend only 40 per cent, therefore we must be understaffed (or, conversely, agency X spends only 40 per cent of its budget on social workers, while we spend 60 per cent, therefore we must be overstaffed). The inconclusiveness of this frequently used line of argument is obvious, for without some statement about (a) the social environment in which X operates compared with us, (b) its objectives compared with ours, (c) its achievements compared with ours, and (d) the other resources available to it, we are in no position to make any sensible inferences whatever. We do not even know whether the differing proportions of total expenditure spent on social workers are due (i) to relatively higher wages being paid by X to people with capabilities similar to ours, and/or (ii) to the employment of relatively better qualified social workers than ours, and/or (iii) to X employing relatively more social workers than we do. And even if we knew all these things, we would still need to know whether their system was more or less productive than ours (i.e. whether it achieved more, in terms of the objectives for which the social workers are employed), and whether there were offsetting cost increases (or decreases) with respect to other associated resources used. Thus this kind of norm suffers from the fact that it is wholly *input* based, and, worse still, concentrates attention on the *money* cost of one *single input*.

1.23 A slightly less crude test would be one concerned with total cost per head of population, e.g. 'in Blankshire they spend £2 per head on home helps for the elderly, while we spend only half that amount'. Again, two distinct inferences could be drawn from that statement as it stands: firstly that Blankshire is providing much better services for the elderly than we are, or secondly, that we are much more 'efficient' than they are. Indeed, the only improvement on the earlier test is that *all* expenditure is now counted, and not just that on a single input.

1.24 Even so, one could go further, even on the input-counting side, because we are still only counting inputs which the agency itself spends money on. There are usually other inputs required which the agency controls but which do not show up in its budget (buildings, for instance, frequently come into this category), or which fall on other agencies' budgets (e.g. co-operating social services), or which represent costs to the agency's clients themselves (e.g. time they spend waiting or travelling). A comprehensive statement of the costs of a social service would need to go beyond the agency's immediate money costs and the account of these broader input notions.

1.25 Things begin to look more promising, however, when we move away from input-based tests to tests which relate to achievement or output. But even here there are traps for the unwary. Pupil-teacher ratios are frequently used as an indicator of quality of education, but on closer inspection these turn out to be ratios between two of the *inputs* into the educational service, and even though they may well be the two most important inputs (books, writing materials, equipment, buildings and transport are others), the pupil-teacher ratio is still not a measure of achievement or *output*.

1.26 Things are only slightly better with tests such as caseload (e.g. number of cases per social worker). Here we are usually involved in a more subtle discussion of an 'optimum' caseload, rather than seeking to make it as large or as small as possible. But, at best, a 'case' is a unit of work, not a unit of achievement, and without any associated measure of 'success' or 'failure' degenerates into a workload (or input-input) indicator rather like the pupil-teacher ratio.

1.27 We take an important step further when we can incorporate success (or failure) measures into our tests, and begin to approach a measure which approximates to 'output per man-hour'. This obviously requires 'output' to be measured independently of 'work done', (e.g. if one could say that an hour of a probation officer's time reduced the risk of x committing a further offence by y per cent then it would be a valid (though limited) test of the probation officer's efficiency. It would be limited because it still centres on a single input (probation officer's time) and does not take into account any associated resources used. By ignoring the latter it implicitly assumes that the associated resources are 'free goods', since this efficiency test leads us to do all we can to improve the productivity of probation officers' time *no matter what this costs* in terms of other inputs.

1.28 This leads inexorably to a formulation of the efficiency test in which the unit to be costed is a true unit of output or achievement, and in which the measurement of costs ranges over all resources or inputs, and not just one 'key' one, nor even just those which have to be paid for out of the agency's own budget. The main conceptual blockage in the way of sensible and relevant efficiency analysis in the social services is the failure to realize this simple truth.

1.29 Even when the conceptual framework is clear, however, we still face daunting practical difficulties in putting efficiency analyses of this kind into effect. These difficulties concern the appropriate notion of output to use in any particular context and how to measure it, and how to assemble the relevant data on inputs, and cost them. But it is sufficient at this stage in the exposition to be clear about the way the problem has to be formulated, because until the right questions are asked, it is futile to expect relevant answers to be forthcoming.

1.210 Those with experience in the social services will doubtless regard the prescription of paragraph 1.28 as a counsel of perfection, as, in one sense, it is. They will say that they have neither the resources nor the responsibility to make perfect decisions in this imperfect world, and that it is all they can do to keep the system from degenerating into chaos. Thus rather than fuss about digging out information on success or failure, on costs falling on clients or on other agencies, their prime responsibility is to look after their own bailiwick.

1.211 It must be regrettably concluded that many social services operate with such a short planning horizon and with such sparse resources that coping with the next crisis is all that those responsible for them feel able to aspire to. But it may well be that it is the very absence of proper efficiency appraisal which has led the agency into that 'poverty trap', and if so it is not sensible to counter our 'counsel of perfection' with their 'counsel of despair'. Fortunately, there is a middle way, for it is quite possible to apply the notions that are being expounded in this book even in situations where one has only limited room for manoeuvre.

1.212 This is just as well, because no one really has unlimited room for manoeuvre, and what is important when setting about reviewing the efficiency of an activity is *firstly* to be clear as to the extent to which you have circumscribed the analysis by taking certain features of the situation as fixed and to make this clear to others too; *secondly* to explore how far these restrictions could be made less stringent given (say) more time to adjust; and *thirdly* to make clear (to yourself and others) what the relative strengths and weaknesses of the analysis are, and what could be done (by further analysis or research) to make good any information deficiencies that have been revealed, so that on the next round (in five years' time?) your successors will not be in the same boat!

1.213 Even though, as is invariably the case, one is not able to do a 'perfect' piece of efficiency analysis, having the ideal rubric in one's head provides one *both* with a set of concepts and relationships (i.e. a calculus) with which to organize one's material *and* with a built-in critical faculty with which to appraise both one's own achievements and those of others. Surely no further justification is needed for treating the efficiency of social services as a serious matter of both intellectual and practical concern to those working, or likely to be working, within them. The outcome, one might add, is a matter of even greater interest to the rest of us as potential clients!

1.3 The calculus in outline

1.31 In order not to bite off more than we can chew at each stage, the efficiency problem has been carved up into easily digestible bits. One object is to show that even in quite limited contexts systematic thinking will protect one from error, enable one to rebut fallacious arguments put up by others, and give clues as to where there may be scope for improving the efficiency of one's own operations.

1.32 Although these are all valuable in themselves, it must be stressed that the calculus does not itself generate better ways of doing things—it only indicates what sort of things are likely to be better, leaving you to seek them for yourself. If you already have ideas about other ways of doing things, the calculus helps you to appraise them. But it is important to recognize that the 'efficiency calculus' is an analytical tool for testing activities out. Tests on cars tell you which are good and bad buys, and why. And although they help car designers improve their models, the testing apparatus is not itself much use for designing cars. So it is with social services. The driving force for the development of new ways of doing things comes from people with creative imagination and a thorough knowledge of the problems. Systematic analysis helps with the latter, and provides a useful directional guide for the former, but more than that it cannot do.

1.33 We shall, therefore, assume throughout that there are existing ways of doing things, and other ways of doing things, without going further into what these are or how one gets to know them. Any alert and imaginative person in a social service agency will be only too keenly aware of such possibilities through the professional journals or through personal contacts or experience. Those who assert that there is no other way than their way of doing things are either of severely limited vision or being obstructive. They may, of course, mean that there is no *better* way than their way, but that is precisely what the efficiency calculus is designed to find out.

1.34 We shall start from a decision context in which an agency has a pre-assigned budget and seeks to do the best it can with the resources thus placed at its disposal. We shall start from the most limited possible room for manoeuvre, and the narrowest conceivable focus of interest, and steadily broaden out. This will have the advantage of simultaneously indicating what is the best course of action within the terms of reference set at each point in time, and of

B

indicating the shortcomings of narrow terms of reference in any efficiency calculus. It will then be for the reader to identify where he or she stands at any point of time along this continuum, and to appraise his or her situation accordingly.

CHAPTER TWO

Provision of District Nurse Services at Minimum Cost

2.1 The problem

2.11 In order to get to grips with efficiency analysis at a practical level, let us start with a homely example which, though simple, contains within it a lot of the problems with which we are concerned. Impatient and sophisticated readers may well consider this apparently naïve (and admittedly oversimplified) starting-point rather a drag. But beware, gentle reader, there is more in it than meets the eye! However, those who can now turn to paragraph 2.31 and immediately understand it can safely skip this chapter. Despite its mainly historical interest and somewhat eccentric institutional framework, the example should nevertheless be recognized by most readers as a particular instance of a much broader class of problems which will be only too common and familiar.

2.12 In a certain rural area there are 39 geographically dispersed clients each requiring the attention of a district nurse once a day. At the moment the district nurse service is provided under the following conditions. The home base is at the county town which is situated roughly in the centre of the area across which clients are scattered. Twelve bus routes radiate from the county town and each client is on or near a bus route. District nurses using public transport can service up to four clients a day, but only if they are all on the same bus route. The bus routes, timetables and geographical layout of the area together conspire to make it impossible for a district nurse to service more than one client unless he or she is situated on or near the same bus route (see Fig. 1, p. 10).

If the situation is as predicted in Figure 1 then bus routes L and E would require one district nurse assigned to each, despite having

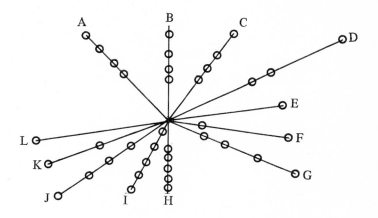

only one client each, while routes I and H with five clients each would both need two district nurses. In all, if every district nurse were to rely on public transport, the clientele of 39 would require a staff of 14.

2.13 The question is this. Given the objective of providing daily visits to all 39 clients who could benefit from the service, is our present way of going about things the most satisfactory? Someone might suggest, 'Wouldn't it be more efficient to provide some of the nurses with cars?' Then we could have them spending more of their time doing what they're trained to do instead of wasting their time sitting in buses or worse still hanging about in all weathers waiting for them. If we could at least provide one or two cars we could amalgamate the more lightly loaded district nurse "beats".' The individual responsible for organizing the service, whom we will anonymously call E, being an intelligent, open-minded individual who would leave no avenue unexplored in the pursuit of efficiency, decides to appraise this change in a systematic way. He knows from a study commissioned by his predecessor that a district nurse with a car can attend *six* clients a day no matter where in the county they may be located. He wants to know how many clients per day can be served with various numbers of district nurses and cars. Since he is bad at keeping things in his head he decides to set out a table with numbers of district nurses along the top and numbers of cars down the side.

TABLE 1

No. of cars	Number of district nurses													
	1	2	3	4	5	6	7	8	9	10	11	12	13	14
0	4	8	12	16	20	24	28	31	33	35	36	37	38	39
1	6	10	14	18	22	26	30	34	37	39				
2	6	12	16	20	24	28	32	36	39					
3	6	12	18	22	26	30	34	37	39					
4	6	12	18	24	28	32	36	39						
5	6	12	18	24	30	34	37	39						
6	6	12	18	24	30	36	39							
7	6	12	18	24	30	36	39							

If he were to use only one car he would be able to dispense with four of the district nurses who had to use public transport. The car-borne district nurse would attend all the clients on bus-routes L,E,F and one on each of I and H. As further cars are added the manpower savings are less dramatic since he would naturally exploit the best opportunities first. The reader is invited to use his ingenuity to see if he can suggest alternative deployments of manpower and cars which would increase the numbers of clients served for any particular level of inputs.

2.14 E now comes to examine his budgetary position. His annual budget is £21,000 which is totally spent on the salaries of district nurses (on average £1,500 p.a.). If he gets a car he can save £6,000 p.a., a not inconsiderable triumph given that his budget is only three and a half times that amount. E does not hesitate. It seems foolish not to adopt this new way of doing things which will perform at least as well as the old way and is at the same time less costly. The provision of cars being the responsibility of the local health executive, E gets on to them right away and orders one, claiming that the new way of doing things would make a material contribution to the efficiency of his operations. The car duly arrives.

2.15 The easy success E scores with this exercise opens the floodgates on his ingenuity. He takes another look at the table of inputs and outputs (i.e. the production function of his operations) that he so carefully devised and sees that a second car will save him a further £1,500 worth of district nurse and so on until the sixth car. But after the sixth car it is no longer possible to substitute cars for personnel as it needs one person to drive each car. E sees that by using cars 2–6 he can save a further three health visitors, i.e. £4,500 in addition to the £6,000 saved by the first car. The decision to use cars has enabled E to halve his costs without any reduction in the number of clients served. E is pleased.

2.2 A snag

2.21 However, trouble is looming. The finance department of the local health executive is not pleased. They feel that E has minimized costs to his own budget only at enormous expense to the health executive budget. They feel E needs a sharp reminder that cars cost money. A suitably cold letter is therefore sent to E inviting him 'to review his need for cars, having regard to the fact that, taking together petrol, maintenance and depreciation, the annual cost of operating a car is £1,000' and continuing, 'We would ask you therefore to justify this expenditure by pointing to corresponding savings in other costs.' E thinks that £1,000 a year to run a car is a bit on the high side but experience has taught him that argument with the local health executive is counter-productive.

2.22 He now sets out to minimize the total cost of his operations taking into account the impact not only on his own budget but also on the local health executive's. Given the costs of personnel and cars E sees that he will have to show that three cars will save at least two district nurses to justify the expenditure, i.e. that one car will save at least two thirds of a district nurse. The first car is now still plainly worthwhile in that it will save four district nurses. So is the second car, since that will save one district nurse. However it requires a further two cars to save one district nurse so that it is plainly not worth it, and the same is true for subsequent increases in the number of cars. E then prunes his demands to two cars and he is able to make do with nine district nurses. He notices that the minimum cost combination of cars and district nurses is also the one at which district nurses saved per extra car is closest to the ratio of the cost of a district nurse to the cost of a car. However, in justifying his choice of inputs to the health executive, E notes down the various combinations of inputs that will suffice to service 39 clients and calculates the total cost of each combination.

TABLE 2

Number of cars	Number of district nurses	Total cost £ p.a.
0	14	21,000
1	10	16,000
2	9	15,500
3	9	16,500
4	8	16,000
5	8	17,000
6	7	16,500
7	7	17,500

2.23 E notes with satisfaction that even taking into account the annual cost of cars, the cost of providing the service is markedly less than it was before cars were provided. Efficiency is up. Where he had erred before was in assuming that since cars did not have to be paid for out of his own budget, they had a zero cost. If cars truly did cost nothing he would have been right to use six, or even seven – even if the seventh car saved no manpower it wouldn't actually bring a fall in the number of clients that could be served. He now sees that the right number of cars will vary according to the relative cost of cars and district nurses. Thus if district nurses were to cost £2,000 it would be worth using a car if it saved half of a district nurse. In our example if the cost of a car is less than half the cost of a district nurse, six cars will be the number that provides the service at least cost.

2.3 Some general principles

2.31 The time has come to set down explicitly the lessons to be gleaned from this experiment in efficient organization. First we need a definition: the marginal product of an input is the extra output that would be produced by adding a further unit of the input to the pre-existing set of inputs (which might of course be no inputs),

Looking back at Table 1, if the pre-existing level of inputs is three cars, four district nurses, producing 22 visits, the marginal product of a further car is two visits. The following general principles were established above:

(a) If one input is twice as expensive as another, then its marginal product must be twice as great to warrant being used.

(b) If the relative marginal products of inputs are not proportional to their relative prices, some advantageous reorganization of inputs is possible.

(c) As relative prices of inputs change, 'efficient' arrangements change, i.e. 'efficiency' is not just a technical matter.

2.4 A further twist

2.41 One final cost-reducing stratagem suggests itself to E. What if, instead of district nurses going to the client, the clients were to come to some central point such as a clinic to receive the service? He unearths some records from 1948 which show that if the district nurse does not have to spend time travelling, she can deal with up to ten clients a day. This means that the service can be provided by four nurses unaided by cars. Thus, the cost of the service can be reduced at a stroke from the minimum (so far) cost of £15,500 to £6,000. From the clients' point of view, however, the service provided is now much worse than it was in that they now have to endure inconvenience and spend time and money in order to avail themselves of it. This will be worse for some than for others, but let us assume that it is the same for all. Whether or not the change is to be made depends upon the valuation E places on the time, convenience and fares of clients. He may seek guidance by eliciting from the clients the value they themselves place on being visited rather than visiting or he may himself postulate a value. He may do this quite implicitly by saying the 'inconvenience to clients is not worth the saving' or even more vaguely 'Clients should not be put to the inconvenience and expense of travelling to a centre.' In any event if he decides not to make the change he is saying that the value of the inconvenience and expense to each client is at least £9,500 ÷ 39 or £243.59. He thus recognizes that the costs to be minimized are not only money costs to the public purse as in the case of cars and district nurses, but also money and non-money costs accruing to any of the parties or agencies involved. If he knew in advance that the yearly cost of cars is £1,000 each and of health visitors £1,500 and of inconvenience to clients who are made to attend a centre is at least £243.59, a grand minimization of costs would lead him to engage nine district nurses and two cars and to visit the clients at their own homes.

2.5 Summary

2·51 To summarize, the pursuit of efficiency within the context of providing a given level of service involves the minimization of the total costs to society of producing the service including the money costs to the decision-maker's own budget, and to any other budgets involved and non-money and money costs to any other relevant party.

Additional Reading

In this chapter we have been expounding elementary production theory, which is common to all economic activity, and is discussed in all standard treatments of economics. The terms 'isoquant' and 'isocost' lines are frequently used in this context. An isoquant line is a set of different combinations of two inputs which will produce the same output—if there are three (or more) inputs we must speak of a plane (or hyperplane) not a line. In the example used in this chapter, 20 visits could be produced by 5 nurses and 0 cars or 4 nurses and 2 cars and these two combinations would be points on a 20-visits isoquant line. An isocost line is the set of input combinations that will absorb a given budget. If a nurse costs £1,500 p.a. and a car £1,000 p.a., a budget of £6,000 p.a. would allow the purchase of the following combinations of inputs: 4 nurses, 0 cars; 0 nurses, 6 cars; 2 nurses, 3 cars and so on. If a particular level of output is to be produced, the correct combination of inputs to use is that for which the isoquant line just touches the lowest attainable isocost line. This is the same rule as 2.31 (b). For expositions of these principles in standard texts see:
R. H. Leftwich, *The Price System and Resource Allocation*, Holt, Rinehart and Winston, 1966, Appendix II to Chapter 7 and Chapter 18, pp. 341–50. Chapter 18 deals explicitly with the problem of indivisibility, e.g. where it is not sensible to talk of fractions of units of input.
P. A. Samuelson, *Economics: an Introductory Analysis*, McGraw-

Hill, Appendix to Chapter 25, 'A Graphical Depiction of Production Theory'.

R. G. Lipsey, *An Introduction to Positive Economics*, Chapter 17, 'Background to the Theory of Supply', especially the section entitled, 'Technical and Economic Efficiency'.

CHAPTER THREE

Choosing the Level of Output

3.1 *The problem*

3.11 In the last chapter we explored the problem of choosing the best mix of inputs, cars and district nurses, to provide a given level of service. Output was therefore fixed. In this chapter we relax the fixed-output assumption and focus on the problem of choosing a level of output for a particular service.

3.12 On a personal note, we record with pleasure that E's abilities have been recognized: he has been promoted to the post of chief purchaser (medical supplies) for Blankshire. Our congratulations are particularly warm because we feel we have played an important part in his success. His first brief is to advise his superiors on a problem that has arisen from the recent introduction of disposable (single-use) versions of many items of hospital equipment such as gowns, aprons, pillow-cases, overalls, sheets, towels, uniforms. The question is how far to continue with the present practice of using durables which are washed in the laundry situated in the Blankshire County Hospital grounds and how far to switch to disposables.

3.13 Since it is not easy to think about output in terms of a motley collection of items like uniforms, towels, sheets, etc. E sets about reducing these heterogeneous items to standard laundry units. The laundry processes the items in batches of a certain maximum weight, so E writes down the weight of each of the items. As his standard unit he chooses the lightest article, which turns out to be a pillow-case, and, on the basis of their weights, expresses every other item in terms of its pillow-case equivalent.

3.14 Next he finds out from the laundry how many of these standard units they process every day. They explain that 8,000 units are dealt with every day and that since laundering is a batch production activity, and not a flow-line activity like car-assembly or whisky-bottling, this is organized into eight batches a day each consisting of 1,000 standard units. From the accounts dept. he discovers that the total daily cost of producing this level of output is £980. Disposables may be had at 10p per standard unit—luckily here too price is proportional to weight so the same standard unit will do for considering both ways of supplying fresh laundry. Reusables are used so many times and their rather higher initial cost spread so much that it can be ignored.* That makes £100 per batch or £800 in all to replace reusables by disposables. The change appears to be worthwhile and the budget £180 to the good.

3.2 *The switch—complete or partial?*

3.21 But a complete switch to disposables means closing down the laundry completely. The accounts department, faced with such a suggestion, points out that the budget would not at all be £180 to the good. Certain contractual payments arising from the construction of the laundry have to be met regardless of how intensively the plant is used or whether it is used at all. When the laundry was built money was borrowed and provision has still to be made to pay interest on the loan and to repay the principal. On a daily basis these payments work out at £100. The true significance of this state of affairs seems to E to be this. Whatever was true when the laundry was being conceived, this £100 is not an *escapable* cost of operating the laundry looked at from today's viewpoint. Given the present upsurge in home washing-machine ownership and the depressed state of the laundry business in general, the laundry's machines and buildings have no re-sale value. No opportunity is forgone by operating the laundry rather than not operating it. E sees that the correct way to view the situation is to ignore these inescapable sunk costs and look upon the plant and machinery as a free good (apart from repairs and maintenance) concentrating attention on the costs that vary with the level of output and ignoring those fixed idependently of it.

3.22 E does the calculation again, this time leaving fixed costs out of the reckoning. Total variable costs of producing eight batches, i.e. labour, fuel, cleansing agents and maintenance is £880, still greater by £80 than the cost of disposables.

3.23 Just at this point E recalls that the laundry always seems to

* Of course, this is unlikely to be true; the assumption is made in the interests of uncluttered exposition.

be humming with activity. Steam is emitted and lights blaze at all hours of the day and night. A conversation with the laundry supervisor reveals that at the high levels of operation current the machines require close watching. Untoward incidents are commonplace. They're always having to stop and de-bug machines. Overtime and Sunday working are common. Plainly output is being squeezed from the laundry at a rate well above what was envisaged in the planning stage. E draws the conclusion that at a lower rate of operation the variable cost per batch might be lower than the £100 implied by a total variable cost of eight batches per day of £880. In order to explore the possibility of working at reduced output E asks the laundry supervisor to produce an estimate of the total variable cost of producing various numbers of batches from 1–10 per day. The information returns in the following form:

TABLE 3

No. of batches per day	Total variable cost (£) (TVC)	Average variable cost (AVC)
1	40	40
2	100	50
3	180	60
4	280	70
5	400	80
6	540	90
7	700	100
8	880	110
9	1080	120
10	1300	130

E calculates a third column showing average variable cost (AVC) per batch i.e. total variable cost (TVC) ÷ the number of batches.

3.24 It is clear that it only requires a cut in production from eight to seven batches a day to reduce the AVC of reusables to the price of disposables, leaving only one batch, or 1,000 standard units, to be provided by disposables.

3.3 A puzzle?

3.31 However when AVC is £100, TVC is £700. Together with the £100 to be paid for a batch of disposables, the laundry budget is £800, exactly what it would be if a total switch to disposables took place. E estimates now what would happen if a further batch were to be replaced by disposables. TVC of six batches is £540; two batches of disposables cost £200. Total cost now is £740, a £60 saving compared with a complete switch to disposables. Although pleased with this result E is rather perplexed. He thought that the correct thing to do was to produce from the laundry until variable cost per unit (AVC) was equal to the cost of disposables. But this decision rule does not lead to the best solution. At the six-batch level AVC is £90, a figure which bears no obvious relationship to the £100 cost of disposables. Further experimentation reveals that the best level of output is four batches of each; cost equal to the TVC of £280 plus £400 for four batches of disposables giving a total of £680.

3.4 A solution

3.41 E decides to go over the exercise again to see if there is a better rule than to push AVC to the point of equality with the price of disposables. Starting at eight batches again, a reduction to seven batches reduces AVC from £110 to £100, but E observes that the reduction in total variable costs is £180. Looking at it another way the cost of an increase in output of one batch from seven batches to eight batches is £180. We may say then that the extra or *marginal* cost of the eighth batch is £180. It is clearly not worth producing this eighth batch if a batch of disposables is to be had for £100. E decides that the correct thing to do is to expand output if the price of disposables exceeds MC (marginal cost) and to reduce output if it is less than MC. Clearly the first thing to do is to write down the MCs of the various levels of output. He discovers that MC of laundering equals price of disposables at four batches, implying the purchase of four batches of disposables, a result that he had already identified as the least-cost solution.

3.42 Even if E had calculated MC from total cost (=TVC + fixed costs) he would have found the result to be the same as calculating

TABLE 4

Batch	TVC	AVC	MC	Total cost (= TVC + Fixed cost)
0	0	0	–	100
1	40	40	40	140
2	100	50	60	200
3	180	60	80	280
4	280	70	100	380
5	400	80	120	500
6	540	90	140	640
7	700	100	160	800
8	880	110	180	980
9	1080	120	200	1180
10	1300	130	220	1400

MC from TVC. Thus adherence to the MC rule alone would have led him correctly to leave fixed costs out of the reckoning.*

3.5 A general principle

3.51 Let us enunciate the main lesson of the hospital laundry example. In determining the best level of output the marginal cost of a unit of the output is the correct decision variable. The decision rule is to expand output if MC exceeds the price of bought-out supplies. If this price should change, output should be altered so as to satisfy the MC equals price rule.

3.6 A value for output—implicit

3.61 E feels that his exploration of the hospital laundry problem has yielded him insights which will be of great value in other branches of the social services. His thoughts naturally turn to his experience

* Change this example by an inch and you have a theory of the profit-maximizing firm operating in a private market setting. If £100 per batch is the price the firm can get for its product sold upon the open market its best profit level of output will be given by the MC = price rule. This footnote is designed, not to betray the insidious commercialism of the authors' reasoning, but to demonstrate the generality of economic principles.

with district nurse provision in his last job but he feels that this is not really like the hospital laundry problem because a fixed output had to be provided and the problem was to minimize costs. He therefore turns his mind to social services where it is not a question of providing a given level of output. He realizes that whatever level of output is chosen in any particular service it will surely be possible to construct a marginal cost curve. That will be half the battle since as he saw from the hospital laundry case, MC was a crucial decision variable.

3.62 There the matter might have rested for ever had not E attended a local health service pow-wow some weeks later. He happens to get talking to an obstetrician and the topic turns to perinatal mortality and its prevention. With a prodigious leap E mounts his hobby-horse. By careful questioning he discovers that the cost of preventing an extra death is now very high, all the deaths which can cheaply be prevented having been prevented. This, E notes, is a case of rising marginal cost, as in the hospital laundry case. 'But how do you know where to stop spending money to prevent extra deaths?' E asks. 'Well,' replies the obstetrician, 'the answer is that you don't. The cut-off point comes where it simply becomes too expensive to prevent a further death.' 'But, how do you mean "too expensive"?' 'It is just not worth the money, I suppose,' replies the obstetrician, his eyes glazing over. Taking his leave of the obstetrician as quickly as decency will allow, E takes an old envelope from his pocket. On the back of it he draws the diagram shown on page 23.

The diagram represents the obstetrician's assertion that after a certain point (on the diagram AB preventions) the extra cost is prohibitive. E sees that the difference from his laundry example is that there is no apparent evaluation of what extra output is worth. In the hospital laundry case extra output was worth £100 per batch, because that is what could be saved by replacing bought out supplies by laundry supplies. But E reasons that the decision to apply a cut-off *implies* that the extra death saved is not worth the extra cost required to save it. If that were not so, if the deaths beyond AB were worth spending more than AC each to save, then rational men would be spending the money and saving the extra lives. E concludes that therefore saving a perinatal death is worth AC to the decision maker. The only difference between the perinatal death case and the hospital laundry case is that in the former case the decision-maker tries to dodge the problem of explicitly placing a value on a life saved and hides behind the device of a cut-off point whereas in the latter case there is an obvious and straightforward

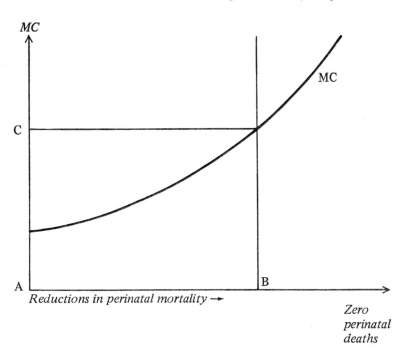

MC

C

A   B

Reductions in perinatal mortality →

*Zero
perinatal
deaths*

method of valuation and the level of output is chosen to be just where marginal cost becomes equal to the value of output. But the result, in the perinatal mortality case, is just the same as if the decision-maker had said: I value a perinatal death saved at AC; we will prevent deaths until the marginal cost of doing so rises to become equal to AC.

3.63 E reflects that this implicit valuation of a life saved was elucidated by observing the marginal cost at which the cut-off was applied. What happens, he muses, if the marginal cost of output is constant, if such a case exists? Conversation with the county's home-help supervisor reveals that such a cost pattern is indeed found in these operations. Home-helps it appears do not operate from a central depot. They appear there once a week to be paid and to be deployed for the coming week but otherwise they operate without supervision and service the clients who live in their immediate neighbourhoods. If need be additional home-helps could be recruited in almost any area of the county. Drawing a fresh envelope from his inside pocket, E jots down the following diagram:

MC

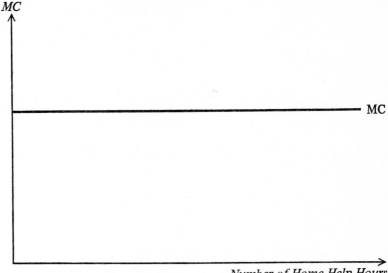

MC

Number of Home-Help Hours

Then he asks the supervisor the crucial question: 'How do you decide when to provide no further home-help visits?' 'Well', she replies, 'we deal with the worst cases first, obviously, but when we are getting down to people who, perhaps with the help of neighbours or relatives, can just about cope then that's the time to halt. If costs got any higher we would cut out the marginal cases and concentrate help on those who really needed it.' This strikes E as a very clear statement of a particular stance. The cut-off comes when the *marginal value* of a home-help visit is just equal to the marginal cost. E sees that the clients' needs must be assigned priorities by the supervisor. Those whose needs seem greatest she places a high marginal value upon, and the marginal value declines as the less needy are reached. This position could be represented by the diagram on page 25 with marginal value expressed in money terms and compared with marginal cost. It is not that the home-help supervisor decides the cut-off point by comparing the two schedules. Rather, in deciding the position of the cut-off she implies a set of marginal values like those in the diagram.

3.64 Any decision to produce one level of output rather than another therefore implies a valuation of the product at the margin.

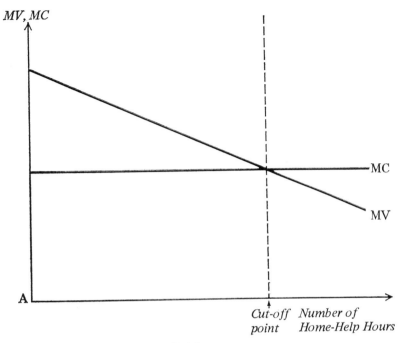

3.7 A value for output—explicit?

3.71 It can be useful to have this valuation in the open rather than under the counter. There are many agencies of government whose activities in one way or another contribute to the saving of lives, e.g. the Department of the Environment in erecting motorway crash barriers; the railways in their choice of level crossing installation; police car patrols as a means of preventing road accidents; the health sevices generally. It is entirely possible that if the implicit valuations of human life in each of these life-saving activities were to be brought out into the open, marked disparities would be found. If it is found to be worth spending £1 million to save a life at the margin by spending on air traffic control equipment but only £5,000 to save a life by putting up pedestrian bridges in villages on main roads, then that means that more lives could be saved by a re-allocation of spending from air traffic control to pedestrian bridge installation. This does not mean that air traffic control should be abandoned and that aircraft should be left to take their chance when landing and taking off. Nor does it mean that every village street should have a pedestrian bridge. It means that money should be spent in such a way that for all ways of saving a life the cost of saving another life should be equal. That way more lives could be saved for a given level of expenditure.

Additional Reading

The problems in the hospital laundry example—what output to produce, under what circumstances to shut down altogether—and the solutions—choose the output at which marginal cost is equal to the price of alternative sources of supply—are analogous, almost perfectly so, with those of a firm which has no influence over the price its products will fetch. See:

P. A. Samuelson, *Economics*, Chapter 22, 'Cost and Supply'.

R. H. Leftwich, *The Price System and Resource Allocation*, Chapter 8, 'Costs of Production', Chapter 9, 'Pricing and Output under Pure Competition'. Chapter 13 ('Pricing and Employment of Resources: Pure Competition') has a little section ('Marginal Physical Products and Marginal Cost') which neatly demonstrates the relationship between our Chapter 2's optimal combination of inputs rule with the marginal cost curve.

CHAPTER FOUR

Output Measurement
in Social Services

4.1 The problem

4.11 Up to this point we have deliberately chosen to skate on some rather thin ice concerning the notion of 'output' for a social service, contenting ourselves with rather homely examples such as 'district nurse visits' as the appropriate unit. This conforms perfectly well with common practice in these fields, and, indeed, with common sense, but it is not an entirely satisfactory notion from an efficiency standpoint, so we must now scrutinize the whole notion of output measurement more closely if we are to make further progress in understanding what 'efficiency in social services' really means.

4.12 We earlier found it necessary to distinguish between a situation in which all visits are of equal value (in which circumstances it is the increasing marginal cost of making visits whch generates the 'cut-off' point on the number of visits undertaken) and the more realistic case in which visits are arranged in some order of priority (in which circumstances there are diminishing marginal benefits from visits as well as increasing marginal costs). In this chapter we look behind this process of arranging visits in an order of priority, and of determining a cut-off point, because they are crucial processes which tend to be accepted too uncritically both by practitioners in the field and by policy makers.

4.13 It must again be stressed that it is not our intention to argue for any particular set of priorities, or to argue that the cut-off points at present being enforced are wrong, or anything like that. Nor are we in a position to assert what the objectives, or priorities, in any particular service, should relate to (e.g. whether meals-on-wheels services *should* concern themselves with anything other than nutritional matters). When we do have occasion to refer to substantive policy matters it will merely be for illustrative purposes, i.e. in order to give the principles some concrete setting. It is for the experts and policy-makers in each field to supply the substantive content to the discussion; our role is merely to set up an appropriate framework within which a properly structured and productive discussion can occur, and in which the risk of error due to ambiguity and confusion is minimized.

4.14 To do this we shall consider some general problems of principle which arise in output measurement in social services. These problems of principle can be encapsulated in three simple questions (which, unfortunately, do not have correspondingly simple answers!), viz:

(i)   What is the appropriate unit of output?
(ii) By whom is it to be valued?
(iii) How is it to be valued?

Each of these questions is interrelated with the others, but in order to make the exposition manageable we shall take them one at a time in the order stated.

4.2 What is the appropriate unit?

4.21 Measuring output is measuring success (or failure). Success (or failure) implies some objective, i.e. something that the agency is trying to achieve. Thus to be 'appropriate', the unit of output must be closely related to the objectives of the agency. Usually agencies have both proximate objectives (like keeping their existing staff fully occupied) and ultimate objectives (like improving the welfare of their clients), while in between are intermediate objectives (like the provision of certain services for clients).

4.22 One of the great pitfalls in measuring the efficiency of social services is to transpose measures unthinkingly from one context to another, for this often leads to nonsensical and dangerously misleading results. For instance, suppose there are 500 beds (='places') in a hospital, and those running it feel that it is wasteful (i.e. inefficient) to have beds empty, so that there will be pressure to maintain a high occupancy rate. If this rate is used as a test of the efficiency of the people responsible for scheduling admissions, and if it is used in conjunction with other tests (such as length of stay) designed to ensure that patients are not being admitted unnecessarily early or kept in unnecessarily long, then it may be a useful first approximation to a measurement of success or failure for that activity in that particular context. But suppose that bed occupancy rates become used as a more generalized test of the efficiency of the hospital service, then we might find ourselves in a situation in which it is being implicitly asserted that the objective of the hospital service is to keep the hospitals full of patients! Things get worse still when such a measure is used as a test of the efficiency of a whole health service, for then the absence of any reference in the 'efficiency' measure to the effects of hospital treatment on the state of the clients is crucial, for it may be that it would be more advantageous (in terms of the health of the patient) to have him treated outside the hospital, even though it meant leaving a bed empty!

4.23 Let us assume, in what follows, that this basic requirement (that the efficiency indicator is properly related to the context of the decision or discussion) has been met, and that we are now interested in exploring the kinds of measures that one could use under each head (i.e. 'proximate', 'intermediate', and 'ultimate'). In any particular case, this is obviously a matter requiring detailed knowledge of the context in which that social service agency is operating, and the objectives set for it, so all we can offer here are some general comments and suggestions designed to stimulate thought and emphasize the basic principles.

4.24 The characteristic feature of 'proximate' indicators is that they tend to relate to levels of provision. They are frequently cast in terms like 'hospital beds per 1,000 population', 'doctors per 1,000 population', 'health visitors per 1,000 population', 'home-helps per 1,000 population', etc. Sometimes the 'per 1,000 population' bit will be made a little more sophisticated by referring only to certain subsets of the population who are 'at risk' (e.g. teachers per child of school age), or by some 'weighting' of population to express the notion that some (e.g. under 5s and over 65s) 'require' a higher level of provisions (e.g. of doctors) than others. One of the main limitations of such measures from an efficiency standpoint is that they deny us the opportunity of considering alternative *modes* of provision which involve different input proportions. For instance, it might be advantageous to reduce health visitors per 1,000 population, but increase the number of cars available to health visitors, so that each one would work more effectively, i.e. increased mobility more than outweighing the fall in the ratio of health visitors to population. Clearly an 'output' measure which 'locks us in' to a particular *input* ratio is not likely to be conducive to 'efficiency', since it shuts out one of the main ways in which efficiency can be improved, namely by changing working methods.

4.25 Intermediate indicators are typically measures of 'through-put' or 'workload'. Here we have 'the visit', 'the treatment', or 'the case' as the characteristic unit. This is clearly an improvement on the 'proximate' indicator, in that it gives us scope for providing for visits, treatments or cases in different ways. But it still leaves some key questions unanswered. We have already become aware of the necessity for establishing priorities among visits, and the same will be true of 'treatments' and 'cases'. Unless the visit is an end in itself (e.g. to establish that the client is still there or still alive) it will usually be associated with some 'treatment' (if only social chat to relieve a sense of isolation), and clients may then be ranked accord-ing to the urgency or effectiveness of these treatments. The same could be said about 'cases', for the agency will normally not be indifferent between the various possible ways in which a case may be 'closed'. In the hospital context it is obviously not a matter of indifference whether the case ends in 'death' or 'discharge', even though some statistics fail to distinguish these two outcomes! Similarly, social workers will regard some outcomes as 'successful' (e.g. the total acceptance of a child into a foster home) and others as 'failures' (e.g. the break up of a family group in mutual antipathy and despair). Thus to appraise the value of these intermediate indicators we have to turn to client state.

4.26 Client state is the characteristic concept underlying 'ultimate' indicators, but unfortunately not *all* client state indicators are ulti-mate indicators in the sense used here. For instance, measures of client need, like 'nursing dependency' scales, are frequently state-ments about *provision*, e.g. so many hours of a nurse's time per day, which only *imply* something about client state, but do not measure it directly. The snag in such indirect measures is that they again lock us in to thinking exclusively about one particular input (like nurses' time) instead of leaving us free to respond more flexibly to the client's state. Thus we are again in the situation described in para-graph 4.24 where what may be a useful indicator for certain limited purposes becomes dangerous when elevated in status. Measures of client state vary from crude indicators like 'alive or dead', through morbidity statistics and social indicators such as crime and divorce rates, to complex social-psychological rating scales to test various aspects of mental state and social functioning at individual level. These are probably as close as it is feasible to get at present to the dimensions of client state relevant to efficiency in social services, and it is to these that we shall return in the last part of this chapter.

4.3 By whom is 'output' to be valued?

4.31 In publicly provided social services we can distinguish a host of 'interested parties' who can legitimately claim that their views on the value of these services should be heard and acted upon. These are the people to whom the services are given; their nearest and dearest; others in the community who 'care' in a rather general and diffuse way about their less fortunate fellow citizens; the people running the service; the politicians and other policy-makers; and last, but not least, central and local taxpayers who finance the services. It is most unlikely that all of them will speak with one voice, so that the question will arise as to whose views shall count most, or, more generally, how conflicts of view shall be resolved.

4.32 We intend to sidestep this crucial question here, because it is a question about political power and influence, and lies outside our terms of reference. But we cannot ignore it, because it has important consequences for the manner in which an efficiency calculus will be pursued. What we propose to do, therefore, is to consider what kinds of things will be of interest to each group in the field of output measurement, so that we have a clearer idea about the nature of the individual ingredients, even though it will be left open what the actual recipe is in which they are to be blended together somehow.

4.33 From this standpoint it will take us unnecessarily far afield to consider all possible interests of all possible parties, so we will concentrate on two of them only, namely 'clients' and 'professionals'. The former group are the immediate potential beneficiaries of the service, and they will stand as proxy for other indirect potential beneficiaries such as relatives and the community at large. The 'professionals' are those with special expertise running the services (social workers, health visitors, etc.) or those closely concerned with them (administrators running agencies, etc.). The interests of politicians as such are considered (idealistically perhaps) to be identified with the 'efficiency' of the services in general, rather than with output measurement in particular, and the same is true of the citizens-as-taxpayers.

4.34 This will leave us with two rival perceptions of what the valuation process is about. The client-originating values are based on the assumption that the clients are the best judges of their own welfare, and that it is their valuations the system should reflect (albeit partially). The professional-originating values are based on the assumption that the experts know best, and it is their valuations the system should reflect (albeit partially). In order to sharpen the issues in what follows, each of these positions will be adopted in turn in an unqualified form. It will be left to the reader to attempt his or her own particular synthesis (if, indeed, synthesis is possible!).

4.4 Valuation by clients

4.41 The commonest mode of seeking client's values is by asking them. It has a lot to commend it, but unfortunately is seldom conclusive, and frequently generates data that is extremely difficult to interpret in terms that help us with our problem. There are two main respects in which 'opinion polling' is often too crude to be useful: firstly, when asked 'would you like X . . .' we are all likely to say 'Yes' if X is likely to be *of any use to us at all*, assuming that we are not going to have to pay for it (or, more generally, assuming that we are not going to have to sacrifice anything else in order to get it); and, secondly, because it is not legitimate to infer from the fact that 80 per cent of respondents answered 'Yes' to X, but only 60 per cent to Y, that X is more highly valued than Y.

4.42 In order to get over these difficulties, we might ask people to place a whole list of things in an order of priority. This too has its weaknesses, of which the two most noteworthy in this context are, firstly, that people are *still* not being put in a position where they face the prospect of sacrificing anything, and secondly, that it will not be clear to us what the priority ordering actually means. To elaborate this last point, if it turned out that *everyone* placed 'the provision of home-helps' above 'the provision of day nurseries', did they mean that *no* day nurseries should be provided until *everyone* has the services of a home-help; or that all extra resources should be put into the home-help service rather than into day nurseries, or that the existing balance should be shifted slightly (how much?) towards home-helps, or what?

4.43 Some still more sophisticated opinion polling has attempted to overcome these problems by giving respondents a notional 'budget' to allocate (in cash or in points) asking them how they would allocate this over a range of possible improvements, each of which has a price tag attached. This has the great advantage that it brings out more clearly the need for choice, and, if carefully designed, will generate information about the rate at which respondents would be prepared to sacrifice one good thing (at the margin) for another. It therefore comes much closer to the reality of the situation than any of the earlier variants.

4.44 This method has another feature which is worthy of note, namely that it gives each respondent equal 'purchasing power' in the relative valuation 'game' (though they are not, of course, in an equal situation in reality). This may be seen as an advantage if what is desired is to get at relative valuations unconstrained by differential real-world purchasing power (other than those which places people where they are), but it will be disadvantageous if it is felt that some people's 'needs' are greater than those of others, and hence their valuations should be given greater weight. Thus it may still be necessary to go through complex processes of reinterpretation to reflect any such judgements that might be made. This brings us much closer to the material of the next section, however, and will not be pursued further here.

4.45 A common objection to all the foregoing means of eliciting people's valuations is that they rely on statements of opinion, and it has been observed that what people say and what people do are often rather different. Where there is a discrepancy between ostensible attitude and actual behaviour, many people would argue that the latter is likely to be a truer indicator of relative values than the former.

4.46 This leads us directly into observing the choices people make in real-life situations, and attempting to infer relative valuations from them. In the simplest instance, if people will not pay the price demanded for a good or service, it is presumed that they value it less highly than the things they *do* buy at that price. Most social services are not charged for in that direct way, so we do not have that kind of information to go on. But it is often the case that people have to expend time and energy (and *some* money) in order to avail themselves of a service (e.g. the bus fare, travelling and waiting time, to go to a doctor's surgery, plus the prescription charge and further time and energy getting some medicine), and it is clear that in many cases people conclude that 'it isn't worth it' and leave minor ailments to clear themselves up, or treat them by (cheaper) self-medication.

4.47 Thus even with nominally 'free' services there are time and money costs which can be estimated and evaluated, and by observing, in a systematic manner, the level of cost at which different sorts of people decide that the service is just worth (or just not worth) having, one can get a rough estimate of the marginal value of that service to those people. As will be seen in the next chapter, it is possible to generalize whole schedules of implicit values in adopting this approach, which can be used just like information on the 'buying' habits of people confronting orthodox 'prices' for goods and services.

4.5 Valuation by 'professionals'

4.51 Those running a social service, and particularly those professionally trained in some relevant field, be it medicine, nursing, teaching, social work probation, or whatever, believe themselves to have some special skill (a) in diagnosing the 'needs' of their clients, (b) in selecting 'treatments' which these clients should undergo, and (c) in assessing outcomes. Each of these claims raises interesting questions, but it is only the last one which is our direct concern here. What we are interested in is *how* professionals judge success or failure.

4.52 Many appear to take the view that it is essentially a 'mystery', into which novitiates can be inducted by some kind of osmosis, but which cannot be communicated to outsiders. This 'cannot be' is not meant to connote professional secrecy, but impossibility. The social worker 'knows' that one child is happy in his foster home and another unhappy, but cannot tell you *how* she knows. This does not seem to be a very convincing stance, and one suspects that it belies an insecure obscurantism designed to prevent systematic analysis of performance. We shall therefore reject it as a statement of principle, though conceding that some things *are* more difficult to measure (and communicate) than others.

4.53 Let us instead start at the opposite extreme, with rather crude and obvious measures of success or failure, and see how far we can get in making them more sensitive without allowing their basis to become obscure. The crudest of them all is the mortality rate, since many social services aim at least to keep their clients alive. This is much used, for instance, in maternity services, where fine comparisons of perinatal mortality rates have been used in arguing that hospital confinements are more efficient than home confinements. Thus, by inference, the prime output of these services is 'reduction in perinatal mortality', and we could then plot against that 'output' the increasing marginal cost of achieving successive reductions as one moves from 'high-risk' to 'low-risk' patients.

4.54 In a less well-articulated manner, probation services (and other connective and supportive services for deviants and delinquents) have been judged by their ability to keep people out of prison, and domiciliary support services for their ability to keep the mentally ill, or infirm, or sick, out of hospitals. This is rather more suspect as an 'output measure', because it relates only indirectly to client state. It is based on the assumption that those who commit further crimes will find themselves in prison, and those who get more ill will find themselves in hospital, neither of which propositions is necessarily true.

4.55 If we return to more direct measures of client state, then morbidity statistics are the next most frequent basis for output measurement. Reducing the incidence of infectious diseases in children, or of non-degenerative conditions in the elderly, or of injuries due to accidents, covers an important realm of activity. Things get somewhat fuzzier with mental illness, especially where the origins lie in inability to cope with the normal stress to be found in a domestic or work situation. But this points to the next important stage in output measurement, where one moves from 'medical' or 'psychological' condition in physiological terms, to general social functioning.

4.56 Here we are in the realm in which it is not the presence or absence of some defined 'underlying cause' which is the relevant test of success or failure, but the ability of the client to function in a working, domestic or recreational context despite it. Thus assessment of physical mobility and manipulative skills, of capacity for self-care and normal social interchange, etc., becomes the key to 'output measurement' over a wide range of social services, which play a supportive and ameliorative rather than an 'exertive' role. Thus the 'output' of the service is to be measured in terms of the independent but effective functioning of the client in his day-to-day activities.

4.57 Since this is frequently multi-dimensional, it is common to employ 'scaling' techniques here, which amount to constructing an *index* as the measure of output. It is important to recognize that in doing this one is *implicitly* engaged in relative valuation of the different items, according to the 'weights' or 'scale points' used. For instance, suppose that 'housing need' is assessed by a points scheme which allots one point for each year on the waiting list; one point for each person after the first two in the household; one point if the existing accommodation occupied has no fixed bath; one point if the number of persons per room exceeds two; etc. Since each of these elements has the same value in the index, this implies that each is as bad as the other in terms of the objectives of housing policy. The same is true of assessment of degrees of handicap, or of loneliness, or any similar dimension which gets 'scored' in this way.

4.58 Indices can, nevertheless, be useful devices for formalizing the process by which priorities are established as between cases, for they make it possible *both* to discuss sensibly whether the relative valuations within the index are appropriate (i.e. whether they reflect the objectives of the service) which is often hard to do if the basis of professional judgements is left obscure, *and* to use index points as rather sophisticated output measures (sophisticated because they represent the outcome of a subtle and complex interplay of elements, unlike the rather crude alive/dead measures).

Thus a well-designed priority rating on housing might generate an index of need which could be aggregated for a given community, and the success of the social services (concerned with improving housing conditions in the area) could be assessed by measuring their impact on this index. In this way such diverse activities as slum clearance and rehousing, rehabilitation of old houses, reallocation of existing housing, etc., could all be brought into systematic comparison with each other.

4.59 All this still stops short of explicit money valuation, though implicit money valuations are still frequently encountered in the form of judgements that at some level of achievement 'going further would be prohibitively costly'. Even this limited statement can be used in efficiency analysis if it is linked with some index which is also relevant to another social service where a different implicit valuation is being made. In such a situation it will be the case that reallocating resources from the agency placing a low value on marginal units of 'index' achievement to that according them a high value will increase the overall level of index achievement. (See Chapter Three, para. 37.1.) However, rather than pursue this line of argument further, it will be more productive to consider what is involved in moving to *explicit* money valuations.

Additional Reading

A good little summary of the conceptual and practical problems encountered in output measurement in the social services is to be found in *Output Measurement Discussion Papers No 2: Personal Services*, IMTA (now CIPFA, 1 Buckingham Place, London SW1E

6HS). Among the other pamphlets in the series is one concerning Public Protection, which is relevant to one of our later concerns.

At a more global level there is an interesting discussion of the problems that arise in formulating general indicators of social well-being which can be used operationally in A. Shonfield and Stella Shaw (editors), *Social Indicators and Social Policies* (Heinemann, London, 1972), which includes chapters on crime, education and health, as well as a more general discussion of problems, and an extensive bibliography. The 'attitudinal' approach is well epitomized by Mark Abrams in his article, 'Subjective Social Indicators' in *Social Trends* No. 4, 1973, HMSO, London, and in an earlier volume in the same series (No. 3, 1972) there is a piece by M. Flynn *et al.* on 'Social Malaise Research: a Study in Liverpool' which explores the possibility of using routine data available at local level to build up indicators of social problems.

The most extensive source of material on output measurement by professionals lies in the wealth of assessment schedules used in 'diagnosis' and 'treatment assignment', either routinely or for research or evaluative purposes. Here the reader will find an excellent survey of the strengths and weaknesses of existing practice, and a promising way forward in S. Fanshel and J. W. Bush, 'A Health-Status Index and its Application to Health-Services Outcomes', *Operations Research*, Vol. 18, No. 6, 1970. Going one stage beyond Fanshel and Bush, and using explicit money valuations, are R. Rosser and V. Watts, 'The Measurement of Hospital Output', *International Journal of Epidemiology*, Vol. 1, No. 4, which has implications well outside the field of hospitals.

CHAPTER FIVE

Money Valuation of Benefits

5.1 Introduction

5.11 In Chapter Three we saw how decisions which were apparently about choosing the level of output of a service actually implied a valuation by the decision-maker of an additional unit of the service. We also saw that if many agencies were each engaged in producing a service, output decisions taken in these agencies might imply different valuations of an additional unit and that adoption of a valuation common to all could bring about an increase in the volume of the service produced without incurring extra cost.

5.12 Now, however, we propose to explore in a much more systematic way the possibility of explicit use of money values for the outputs of social services. One major advantage of having the output valued in money terms is that it is commensurable with the input since costs can be, and normally are, expressed in money terms. With a points index this is not possible, for the most that can be said is that an additional expenditure of £x will raise the index by y points, and there is no way in which it is possible to decide whether £x is greater than y points or y points exceed £x, whether in short it is worthwhile to spend £x. The most we can say is that the value of the index (number of points) should be maximized for any given expenditure of money or that the money cost of attaining a given level of the points index should be the minimum; but we cannot decide the scale of the operation.

5.13 There are two main sources for the money valuation of outputs:

(a) they may be taken as the values to the beneficiaries of the service. Just how these are to be elicited is an important concern of this chapter.

(b) they may be postulated by 'experts' or decision-makers (e.g.

the Minister of Transport may fix the value to be placed on lives saved by improved road safety).

5.2 Valuation by beneficiaries

5.21 We have to make an oblique approach to the problem of consumers' valuations of what they consume by first of all considering a simple theory of consumers' behaviour. The rational consumer with a certain income at his disposal will spend it on various goods and services in such a way as to get the greatest satisfaction he can from that income. From this it follows that the consumer will allocate his expenditure among goods and services so that the satisfaction derived from the last penny spent on each is equal. If a consumer's marginal valuation (MV) of a commodity is defined as the amount of money he would be willing to give up in exchange for a further unit of the commodity, it follows that he will continue to purchase further units until his MV equals the price charged per unit. Therefore, for example, if we knew the consumer buys ten pints of milk per week at 5p per pint, then we can say his MV of the tenth pint is 5p.

5.22 We could build up a consumer's MV schedule for, say, tea in the following manner. Considering a time period of one week, what would the price have to be before the consumer would just be willing and no more to buy one cup of tea? The answer might be 20p. In that case, 20p would be the consumer's MV of the first cup. Next we could ask what the price would have to be before the consumer would just be willing and no more to buy two cups of tea. The answer might be 16p and that would be the consumer's MV of the second cup of tea. By successive questions of this kind we might build up the following table of information:

Number of cups of tea	1	2	3	4	5	6	7	8	9	10	11	12
MV of each cup of tea	20	16	13	10	8	6	5	4	3	$1\frac{1}{2}$	$\frac{1}{2}$	0

We could represent this information in graphical form as shown on page 40. The graph tells us how many cups of tea the consumer will choose to buy at any given price. At a price of 9p, for example, the consumer will buy four cups of tea because the MVs of the first four cups exceed 9p, whereas his MV for the fifth and subsequent cups is less than 9p. He would lose more than he gained by buying the fifth cup. If the tea were free the consumer would push his consumption

D

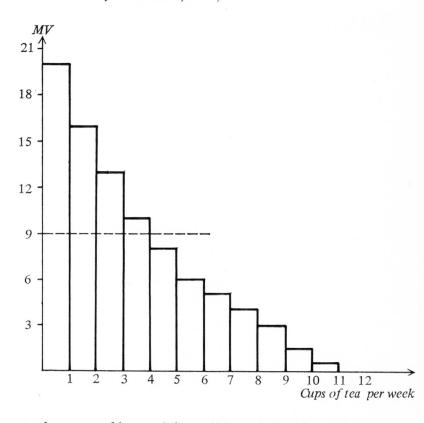

to eleven cups, his MV of the twelfth cup being zero. In general the consumer will continue to purchase units of a commodity until his MV equals the price he has to pay.

5.23 This simple proposition at once yields us an enormous amount of information. Once we know the price of a commodity we at once know every consumer's MV for the commodity, irrespective of his circumstances. Why is this? Because the price is a measure of the sacrifice the individual has to make to obtain the commodity. We therefore know that if the price is 5p, 5p is what the marginal unit is worth to the consumer. Look at the two related diagrams below which depict the MV curves of two different persons for one commodity. Since the commodity in question is readily divisible into small units, the curves are drawn smoothly continuous, rather than in steps:

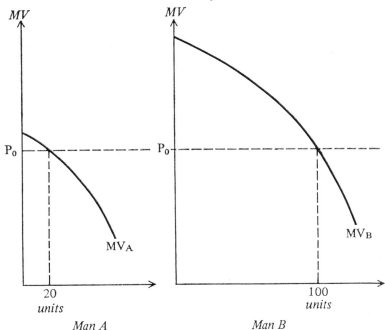

Man A   Man B

The price both must pay for the commodity is Po. Man B's MV curve lies further out than man A's to represent the fact that at any price man B is willing to buy more of the commodity than man A. The reason may be that B is richer than A or just that he has more taste for the commodity. But, although at price Po B buys five times as much as A, *their marginal valuations are exactly the same* since both are led to buy units of the commodity to the point where MV equals price.

5.24 Let us enunciate this important truth: if every consumer is faced with the same price for a commodity, then every consumer's MV of that commodity will be the same, and equal to the price.

5.25 As a result of this piece of elementary economic theory we are given access to more information and more accurate information about people's valuations of goods in the real world than we could get from a flood of Gallup Polls and a deluge of social surveys.

5.26 The proposition that MV equals price needs to be broadened out somewhat. We have so far assumed that money is the only thing consumers have to give up in order to obtain a good or service. This, of course, is untrue. Consumers may additionally have to give up other things that they value such as time, comfort and convenience. If I wish to travel from London to Paris, we can say that being in Paris is the service I wish to buy. The cost of the service is not only the train and boat fare. I will certainly have to use up some time which I might use to advantage in other ways and I may suffer the discomfort of *mal de mer* on the Channel crossing. These non-monetary costs which I have to undergo have a money value to me, since if I were offered the chance of being conveyed instantaneously and without discomfort from London to Paris I might be willing to pay well in excess of the train/boat fare. My behaviour might then be said to imply that the time and discomfort saved was worth at least the money value of the difference between the boat/ train fare and the fare for instantaneous conveyance.

5.27 But there are also circumstances in which the *only* sacrifice the consumer has to make to obtain the service is non-monetary. In order to visit his doctor the patient only has to find the time and undergo the convenience of getting there. Clearly this cost will be much greater for some than for others. To the hard-pressed executive of popular legend the opportunity cost of a visit to the doctor will be very high in that the productive value of the time devoted to other uses will be high. He is likely to substitute self-medication or postpone the visit. Old age pensioners with little to occupy their time on the other hand might be glad of a visit to the doctor as a means of filling the day in a purposive way. The 'price' of a visit is therefore low This is why doctors' waiting rooms are occupied by the old, the un- or non-employed and empty of highly-paid executives to an extent that cannot fully be explained by differences in their proneness to ailment. It is clear that if the costs of using a service are principally time and convenience, there is no reason why everyone's M V for the service should be the same.

5.28 The reader might reasonably expect that at this point the authors would go on to reveal how a M V schedule for some 'free' social service might be built up which would stand comparison with the M V schedule for tea presented earlier in this chapter. This is by no means always necessary. Often the problem in practice is to appraise some minor prospective change. Returning to Chapter Two, we might be faced with the problem of whether to require clients to come to a clinic or to have district nurses visit the clients. In Chapter Two we generated information on the extra costs to the public purse of visiting clients. Now we want to elucidate clients' valuations of the time involved in visiting the clinic. The short answer is that it is quite possible to develop sets of values which different people place on time in different circumstances. It is not possible to undertake a direct investigation into how clients would value the privilege of being visited rather than having to visit the clinic since there is no direct market in which they can express their preferences. But in other circumstances it has been observed how people trade money off against time, e.g. by choosing to take a bus rather than walk or by driving a geographically longer but quicker route (trade off between money spent on petrol and time) or how they would pay a bridge toll rather than take a longer route to avoid the toll. These values of course will vary according to the income, employment status, age of the subject and the nature of the time saving, e.g. time might be valued more highly during work hours than during leisure, higher in the morning than in the evening, higher during the week than at the weekend; and it might change with the length of the saving, e.g. a whole hour saved might be worth more than 60 separate minutes saved. Thus, taking the figures of Chapter Two, if the value of time to clients exceeds £9,500 p.a. then the district nurses should go to the clients.

5.29 However, in certain cases it *is* useful to have an entire MV schedule for a particular service. Suppose the central library of a medium sized town is being replaced. The question may arise whether there should be one large centrally situated library or whether a whole set of libraries should be built in local shopping centres. Here we are not thinking of measures involving one or two more trips to the library. The mooted change involves appraisal of different ways of providing the whole block of visits to the library.

5.210 How would we build up the MV schedule for the main library? We would have to find the money value of what clients were prepared to sacrifice. If we did have a price based on travel cost and the value of time, we would observe that people would be faced with different prices according to their distance from the library. This is how we get the variation in price necessary to build up a schedule. We might divide the catchment area of the library up into a series of areas in order to reduce to manageable proportions the number of individual sites considered. The distance to the library from an area would now be the distance from the centre of the zone to the library. A survey of library users might reveal the following relationship (p. 44) between price and trips per 000 population.

5.211 If we assume that those living in zone A near the library would behave like those in zone Z far removed from the library if faced with the same 'price' for using it—which seems a reasonable

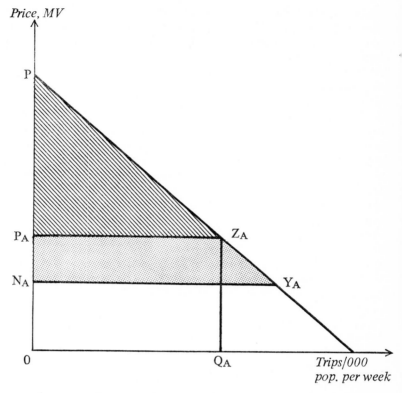

Price, MV

enough assumption—we may assume that the schedule we have is an MV schedule for all zones. From this curve we can find the total net value placed on having a library by the residents of, say, zone A. Zone A residents have to pay a price of OP_A to use the library. However, it is only the last trip undertaken that they value at OP_A: the MV of the OQ_Ath trip is OP_A. The first trip is valued at OP, the maximum anyone would be prepared to pay if allowed to visit the library only once a week. Yet the price of the first trip is only OP_A. Therefore, on the first trip consumers gain a surplus of PP_A, the difference between their valuation of the trip and what they have to pay to make it; on the final trip undertaken surplus is zero since on that trip MV=price. For trips between the first and OQ_Ath the general rule still holds that surplus equals MV minus price. For a smoothly continuous MV schedule such as the one above, total surplus from the library is the shaded area PP_AZ_A.

5.212 When we were thinking about the MV schedule for tea we could have undertaken a similar exercise. If tea is sold at 9p, the surplus on the first cup is 11p, on the second 7p, on the third 4p and on the fourth 1p, making 23p in all. However, the consumers' surplus is unlikely to be relevant to any problem involving tea since tea is made available in small units. It would only be relevant if we were thinking of bribing people to abstain from tea-drinking altogether, in which case the bribe would have to exceed 23p per week for the individual whose schedule is depicted at the beginning of this chapter.

5.213 Returning to the library problem, a dispersion of library sites would lower the 'price' for every zone. If we consider only zone A, price might fall to ON_A Consumers' surplus from the new facility would be PN_AY_A; consumers' surplus from the *change* in library location would be surplus from the new facility less surplus from the old or PN_AY_A—PP_AZ_A, that is the stippled area $P_AN_AY_AZ_A$. If the relevant measure of the benefit from the change is only that strip, why do we need the entire MV schedule? The answer is that for some zones, say zone Z, a rural area some distance from the town centre, OP_Z, the 'price' of getting to the central library, might be in the neighbourhood of OP, the price at which no visits take place. Thus the relevant stippled area might be something like PN_ZY_Z, the measurement of which obviously requires knowledge of the top end of the MV schedule (see diagram, page 46).

5.214 To find out the total value of the benefit of the change multiply the stippled area which is of course expressed in money terms for each zone by the number of 000s of population in each zone and sum over all zones. The change is worth making if the benefit suitably aggregated over time, exceeds the cost differential of dispersed over centralized distribution points.

5.215 Of course, in practice an appraisal of the change would be much more complicated than this, particularly in view of the fact that to split a central library into several branches might well reduce the attractiveness of the individual branch in terms of availability and variety of the book stock. But the method outlined here would also be useful as a means of appraising a change in location of a central library, or a merging of several branches. And in general these principles are worth keeping in mind when it is a question of clients travelling to a centre.

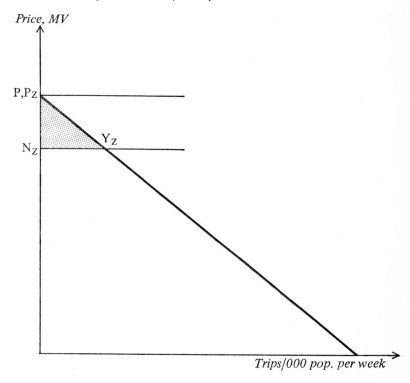

5.3 *The relevance of consumers' surplus*

5.31 It will have been noted that we have slipped into the habit of talking in terms of 'consumers' surplus'. Perhaps it is time to offer a word of explanation of this important idea. The layman is no stranger to the *concept* of consumers' surplus, although the terminology will be unfamiliar. When people say, 'What would we do without the dustmen?' an utterance that may be prompted by dustmen's threats of a withdrawal of labour, what they are really saying is 'Our total valuation of the services of dustmen is very high while the charge for their services is comparatively low', and this is a statement about consumers' surplus. If households were charged £1,000 per annum for refuse collection services, few would derive any surplus from the service, since most would make their own arrangements for refuse disposal. At that price, few would miss the dustmen.

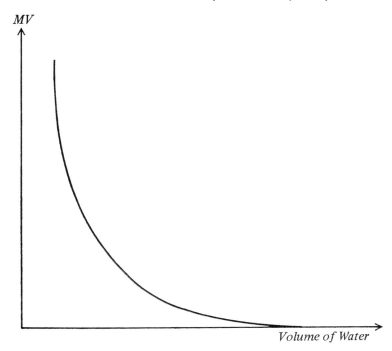

MV

Volume of Water

5.32 But there are other circumstances in which laymen use surplus concepts. Where consumers' MV's of the first few units of a good or service are infinite, implying that we cannot do without at least some of the commodity, the layman is often inclined to use surplus concepts. Water is a case in point. An individual household's MV schedule for water might look like this: The first few pints are valued highly because they are necessary to sustain life. Subsequent units are devoted to less urgent uses—operation of WC's, washing one's person, clothes, crockery, the car, watering the garden, filling the swimming pool. Given the considerable scope for low-priority use of water, the MV curve has a long low tail. Now although households have to pay a price for water through their water rates, this price is not directly related to the amount of water they use. Since there is no extra charge for using an extra gallon of water we may say that it is free to consumers at the margin. With a zero marginal price water will be consumed till every household's MV for it is zero, a principle we established at the beginning of the chapter. In the extreme the consumers' surplus from water is

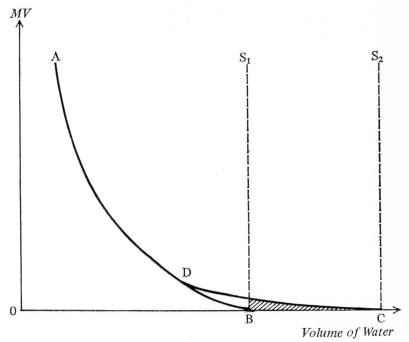

Volume of Water

infinite, since individuals' MV schedules start at an infinitely high level, yet marginal value is zero.

5.33 We can easily develop an aggregate MV curve for water if we know the MV curves of all individuals: for each level of MV add together the amounts of water corresponding to that level of MV for every individual. Suppose we have such an aggregate schedule. Call it AB. Consumption of water is OB. We will assume that supplies of water (represented by BS_1) exactly meet a demand of OB. Over time, however, as households become more affluent their consumption of water for low-priority uses (like garden-watering, car washing) increases, let us say to OC. Over the stretch AD the curves are identical since basic water needs do not increase with rising incomes. The new MV curve is ADC.

5.34 What the authorities responsible for water supply observe, or more strictly, predict, is a rise in water 'needs' from OB to OC. They then set themselves assiduously to scouring the Ordnance Survey maps for sites to build a new set of reservoirs, no doubt stirring up a veritable hornet's nest of farmers and conservationists. What is rarely suggested is that the investment needed to produce the BC extra water supply should not be proceeded with. Against such a suggestion we might typically hear arguments such as, 'The reservoirs must be built because water is the one thing we cannot do without.' That is to say, the consumer's surplus from water is infinite. The assertion is true but irrelevant. No one is suggesting that all water supplies should be withdrawn, only that an increase in the expressed demand should not be met. With the new aggregate MV schedule ADC, an increment in the water supply of BC yields a consumers' surplus of only the cash amount represented by the shaded area, and this is likely to be small since we are in the region of the MV schedule's long, low tail. Against that gain to consumers must be set the cost of the programme of new reservoir construction. If, as we have suggested may happen, the cost swamps the consumers' surplus, then this extra water is something the community not only can do without but would be better off without since the resources could be employed to produce other goods or services upon which consumers place a higher valuation. Of course, if it was decided not to build the reservoirs, a method would have to be found to choke off the excess demand so as to eliminate low-priority uses, to make sure that Mr. B's taps do not run dry because Mr. A decides to water his tomatoes. That, however, should not be beyond human ingenuity.

5.35 In the preceding water supply example the confusion was not between consumers' surplus and valuation of a marginal unit, but between the consumers' surplus to be derived from two district blocks of output. The error was in appraising the value of block BC in terms of the consumers' surplus derived from the block OB. Since a whole block of output is being considered, however, consumers' surplus is still the correct method of valuation. The following example based on opinion polling, however, may demonstrate how easy it is to confuse consumers' surplus and marginal valuation. Suppose you were asked in an opinion poll the unlikely question 'Do you prefer tea or coffee?' Your answer might depend on your interpretation of the choice you were being offered. If you interpreted the question as 'Which would you give up if compelled to do so?' you might decide to retain tea and dispense with coffee, since at price OR per cup (Diagram 2), consumers' surplus from coffee (shaded area in Diagram 2) is less than the consumers' surplus from tea (price OQ per cup; surplus the shaded area in Diagram 1). On the other hand if you construed the question as 'If you were to be given a free cup of tea or coffee, which would you take?' you would choose the beverage for which your valuation at the margin (i.e. at OA cups

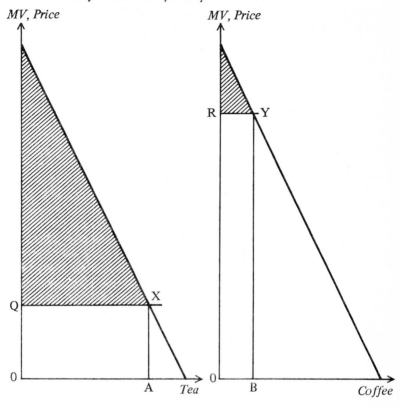

Diagram 1   *Diagram 2*

of tea and OB cups of coffee) was greater, i.e., coffee, since no off-setting price was being exacted. Finally, if you interpreted the question as 'Which will you buy next, tea or coffee'? you might well be indifferent between the two since your MV was already equal to price in both cases.

5.36 Trivial though this experiment may seem, only slight changes are needed to transform it into something more significant. Suppose the question asked was 'Are home-helps more important than day nurseries?' You might have (vaguely) in mind MV schedules for both services (perhaps on behalf of clients) and MC schedules and these might be depicted on diagrams much like 1 and 2 immediately above. Your answer might then similarly depend on what you thought was the actual choice. The problem is that people often think about small prospective changes in levels of service in terms of the total net value of the service. They might pose questions about whether day nurseries or home-helps were to be expanded in terms of the total net value of the presently produced level of service. It is always important to be clear when appraising small changes in output to think only of the costs and benefits associated with the small range that is relevant and to ignore the valuation (benefits) and costs of the vast block of output which is not being appraised, for these benefits and costs are irrelevant and misleading.

5.37 Finally, the reader should be aware that a most constructive use of the questionnaire approach has been developed. In a previous chapter we alluded to a type of questionnaire in which the respondent is given a fixed imaginary budget to 'spend' on a number of items in a list, the objective being to lead him to reveal his valuations. There are two major ways of using this technique:

(i) Give the respondent a notional increase in wealth to be spent on a fixed number of good things to see how he trades one off against the other, e.g. in one instance respondents were 'given' £1,500 extra to 'spend' on certain attributes of house location such as freedom from fumes, noise, traffic, and certain kinds of pedestrian safety and parking nuisance.

(ii) Without 'adding' to the respondent's budget face him with a wider range of choices than he normally has. For example, observation of the choices people make between spending time and spending money is often a blunt instrument for eliciting the value they place on time since they may only be able, say, to choose walking or going by bus. What we might want to know, however, is how much they would be prepared to pay for a five minute reduction in bus journey time or a ten per cent increase in service frequency. So, simply present the consumer with a finer gradation of choices within the *actual* budget constraint and you get far more information about actual valuation than is possible by mere observation of behaviour.

5.38 The first method requires careful handling. The greater the notional increase in the budget and the smaller the choice set on which it is to be spent the less helpful will be the results. The *reductio ad absurdum* might be to increase the respondent's budget by £10,000 all to be spent on different varieties of peanuts. There are two dangers: (a) if the respondent were actually £10,000 better off he might not spend the whole lot on peanuts; (b) even if before and after he receives the extra money he does consume peanuts, he might not consume the varieties in anything like the same proportions. Danger (b) can be mitigated, if not overcome, by performing the exercise of making a corresponding reduction in the budget the consumer devotes to the variables in question, with the object of bringing to light what he dispenses with in cutting his coat according to the smaller cloth. Then an average of this with the choice with the increased budget might more accurately reveal the consumer's trade-offs between the variables at his current income.

5.39 The second method has dangers if the client feels that (a) the questionnaire forms part of a study to determine whether it is worthwhile for, say, the local authority to increase the frequency of the bus service and (b) there will be no corresponding increase in fare, any deficit being covered out of increased general taxation in which his own share is negligible. Then the respondent is being offered something for nothing and he has an incentive to place a high value on the improvement if he values it at all, or, if a notional price tag is attached, to declare himself willing to meet the price whether he is or not.

5.4 Postulated values

5.41 So far in this chapter we have been discussing ways of eliciting the subjective valuations of consumers of the social services. Markets operating on commercial lines automatically generate this sort of information. We have therefore sought implicit or stimulated market situations where consumers do make sacrifices which we can value for goods and services which are not explicitly priced. Although we may bemoan the lack of the ready information which explicit markets provide, this must not be interpreted as covert advocacy of markets in the present context. It is because of certain undesirable features of markets that we choose not to operate in that way in the social services.

5.42 But what is to be done if these surrogate market devices fail us? One long stop is to examine the evaluations implicit in policy decisions in other (related) areas. Put crudely, the justification is that the decisions of public policy-makers must embody the valuations of their electors, otherwise they would not have been elected. One snag with this line of argument is that when electors choose governments they have to vote for a whole package of measures, not just for, say, the valuation to be placed on saving life. Still, there may be nothing better. So if we want to know the value of life for health service purposes, we might examine ministerial decisions on road safety. If the minister is prepared to spend (implicitly) £30,000 per life saved but not £50,000, that is a useful and revealing piece of information. But it is equally likely that road safety might look to health for such valuations, or that both might look elsewhere. For example, society is prepared to make transfer payments to keep people alive who, through old age for example, would be unable to subsist on the product of their own efforts. The maximum such sum is clearly the least it would be worth spending, since society might countenance larger transfers if these were needed. Another possible source of society's valuations is court settlements. Is the compensation an injured employee is awarded society's valuation of the injury? Courts tend to give weight to loss of earning power and are less concerned with pain, grief and suffering: they latch on to what is readily measurable. (However, an example of the use of court awards is given in 7.4, pp. 71–4).

5.43 It should also be remembered in this context that, as we pointed out in Chapter Three (3.6, pp. 21–5) decisions about cut-off points of themselves imply valuations of the output of the service, though in this case the valuations are those placed by the decision-makers on the benefits received by clients, which may not be the valuations of the clients themselves. It is nevertheless useful to bring these proxy valuations into the open if only to discuss whether they are appropriate, and if so to ensure their uniform application.

5.44 Even if consumers' valuations are easy to elicit, society may wish to override them. In such a case the obvious thing to do would be for the policy makers to postulate a valuation to be used in all planning decisions. If this valuation is expressed in money terms it is on all fours with items valued by other methods, e.g. by eliciting the implicit subjective values of consumers. Indeed, the point of having all values expressed in money terms is that they can simply be added up. For example, in road investment appraisal the value of time saved (expressed in pence per minute), which will probably be a value distilled from an implicit market situation, is to be added to the value of lives saved, even though this may be a ministerial valuation which overrides the valuations of road-users as revealed in their behaviour on the roads.

Additional Reading

Exposition of consumer behaviour theory in terms of the marginal valuation as opposed to the demand schedule is relatively modern and our practice is like that found in A. J. Culyer, *The Economics of Social Policy*, Martin Robertson, 1974, Chapter 2, pp. 17–22. An explanation of the concept of consumers' surplus using MV terms is to be found in E. J. Mishan, *Cost-Benefit Analysis*, Allen & Unwin, 1971, Chapter 7. Development in Chapters 8 and 9 is rapid. For a more traditional textbook exposition of demand theory see R. G. Lipsey, *Positive Economics*, Chapter 7, 'The Elementary Theory of Demand'. The demand curve can for most purposes be looked upon as an MV curve. A good elementary insight into consumers' surplus can be gleaned from P. A. Samuelson, *Economics*, Chapter 21, 'Theory of Demand and Utility', section entitled, 'Consumers' Surplus'. This involves less than two pages of text!

CHAPTER SIX

Money Valuation of Costs

6.1 Cost=opportunity forgone

6.11 The reader may be forgiven if he finds it strange that we should have followed a chapter entitled 'Money Valuation of Benefits' with a chapter on the 'Money Valuation of Costs', particularly if he recalls that one main reason we advanced in favour of an attempt to place a money value on benefits was to achieve commensurability with costs which *were* expressed in money terms. This chapter then is intended to serve to bring together some strands of thought which have already appeared as well as to introduce something new.

6.12 Economists' notion of cost is probably rather different from that of the layman. For economists the cost of doing something is the value of what is forgone in order to do it. Often the idea of forgoing something is stressed in the phrase 'opportunity cost'. It is plain that this is a much broader notion than the expenditure of money. An activity may have a high opportunity cost and no yet money changes hands at all, e.g., if a manufacturing firm owns the city-centre site on which it operates, it will not pay for using it in the sense of money being handed over, cheques remitted etc., but other firms might be willing to pay a great deal for such a central site since it might be for them a very productive input, so much so that it might pay the manufacturer to sell the site and move to a suburban location. But a more fundamental grasp of opportunity cost will result if we rip aside the veil of money altogether. For the individual consumer, if a pint of beer costs 20p and a cinema seat costs 40p, then the cost of the beer is half a cinema seat, and the cost of a cinema seat is two pints of beer. The same holds good when society faces decisions on how to allocate resources. If a given quantity of inputs can be used to produce three primary schools

E

or one general hospital, the cost of the hospital is three schools, or the cost of a school is one-third of a hospital.

6.13 However, money has great merit as a *measure* of opportunity forgone. When deciding whether to build a hospital or not it would be very difficult to go through the huge list of alternative good things that might be produced by the resources needed, e.g. twenty miles of motorway, a new university, a hundred cars, ten bingo halls, ten million needles and so on. So the money cost of the inputs of labour, machinery etc., is used as a measure of what is forgone. Why is that a measure of what is forgone? The reason is to be found in the input purchasing policy of producers. Producers will continue to purchase an input until the value of what is produced by the input is equal to the price of the input. Now we have already seen that at the margin consumers' valuation of the goods they buy is equal to their price. Thus the price that has to be paid to secure inputs is a measure of consumers' valuation of what the inputs might otherwise be used to produce.

6.14 It is important to bear in mind, however, that there are circumstances in which (a) the price that has to be paid to secure inputs exceeds the opportunity cost of using them, and (b) there may be no price exacted for using inputs in some prospective way though there may be an opportunity cost. The following examples are intended to illustrate these two claims. They by no means exhaust the possibilities. Once the principles involved have been grasped, however, the acute reader will no doubt be able to think of other examples for himself.

(a) When a hospital is being built labour has to be attracted from other uses. An increase in the number of bricklayers used on the hospital site means a decrease in the numbers available for other building purposes. However, in circumstances where bricklayers are unemployed, the hospital can be built without affecting supplies of bricklayers available at other sites. No alternative goods are forgone, though the bricklayers of course have to be paid the going rate. The opportunity cost of hospital brickwork is therefore the subjective value to bricklayers of lost leisure, which is likely to be small and can for all practical purposes be ignored.

(b) If we cast our minds back to the reusables versus disposables problem we will recall we appraised the change on the basis of the levels of monetary outgoings from the hospital and its laundry only. However, it is conceivable that the decision could have effects on other agencies. For example, a switch to disposables might cause such a vast increase in the hospital's daily refuse output as to require extra trips from the refuse vehicle. This would impose real costs on the refuse collection services in terms of fuel, labour and land on which to dump refuse. These costs are true opportunity costs since the resources involved have other uses. When one decision-making unit imposes costs (or confers benefits) on another unit without having to take them into account itself the situation is said to give rise to an externality. Externalities are very pervasive and are the subject of much popular (and even fashionable) discussion. If a power station uses the air as a dump for its smoke and ash it is imposing an externality on individuals who may later have to breathe the resulting gas. This book could be filled to bursting with the problem of externalities. Here, however, we content ourselves with a reminder that the true opportunity costs of an activity will not be measured by its money costs if externalities occur.

Lest the reader be plunged into gloom by this section, let us also make clear that positive externalities occur too: if I have apple trees and my neighbour is a bee-keeper it is likely that we will confer external benefits on each other.

6.15 These are only two examples of circumstances in which money costs require modification if they are to reflect opportunity costs. There are many other instances. The golden rule is always to think in terms of the opportunity forgone and to ask 'Is this or that payment an accurate measure of the value of the opportunity for gone looked at from the point of view of society as a whole?'

6.2 Comparing costs and benefits over time

6.21 Finally, we turn to a problem which affects both costs and benefits alike. It is the problem of comparing streams of costs and benefits over time. When we were considering the hospital laundry problem we assumed that the stock of plant and equipment was fixed. Now it is time to focus attention on the decision to invest in plant and equipment. The essence of the investment decision is time. Capital equipment such as factories, machinery, roads, hospitals, schools, airports, railways can be combined with land and labour to produce benefits for many years. Yet the outlay must be made typically over a much shorter time. The question is how to compare an outlay of £x now with a stream of benefits of £y per annum for the next ten years. The method is to convert any stream of costs and benefits to a lump sum present value.

6.22 Let us suppose an agency, say a hospital laundry, is considering whether to install an £800 machine which is expected to last for ten years and to yield, net of all payments to cooperating inputs, a return of £100 in each of these years. Summing the yearly return over the ten years gives £1,000. This looks good against a purchase price of £800. But is it?

6.23   In answering this question it is important to realize that the funds to pay for the machine will normally have to be borrowed at a price, conventionally expressed as an annual percentage—the rate of interest. Let us suppose the rate of interest to be 10 per cent. Suppose we borrowed £100 at a 10 per cent rate of interest compound, agreeing to repay both interest and principal in three years' time. The amount owed will be £110 after one year, £121 after two years, and £133.10 after three years. Thus if A is the original sum (£100) and i is the rate of interest (10 per cent or 0·1), the value of the sum is $A(1+i)$ after one year, $A(1+i)^2$ after two years, and $A(1+i)^3$ after three years. The basic formula for *compounding* is $A(1+i)^n = B$, where n is the number of years into the future you wish to go, and B is the sum you will owe then (in this case £133.10).

Interpreting this a little differently we could have asked, 'If you were offered £133.10 in three years' time, and the interest rate is 10 per cent, what is the minimum sum you would be prepared to accept *here and now* as equivalent to it (ignoring uncertainty, inflation etc.)?' Obviously, you would regard £133.10 in three years' time as equivalent to £100 now, because at an interest rate of 10 per cent you could convert £100 now into £133.10 in three years' time, so it shouldn't matter. Thus £100 could be said to be the *present value* of £133.10 in three years' time at 10 per cent rate of interest. Thus the calculation of *present values* is simply the calculation of compound interest done *backwards* in time instead of forwards in time and the formula is therefore

$$A = B \frac{1}{(1+i)^n},$$

where A is said to be the present value of B (and the value of A obviously varies according to the values of i and n).

6.24   Suppose now that a public agency has the opportunity to buy a piece of equipment costing £100 which will save costs of £121 at the end of a year, and is useless thereafter. Applying the above formula we find that the present value of the cost saving is £121/1.1 = £110. The agency is £10 to the good in present value terms. Clearly, if 10 per cent is the rate of interest (or rate of discount as it is sometimes called), it is worthwhile for the agency to spend up to £110 now if that will save £121 at the end of a year. A small extension of the principle will enable us to appraise an opportunity which has a yield in more than one year. Suppose a £100 outlay will result in a return of £60.50 at the end of year 1 and £60.50 at the end of year 2, and zero thereafter. The conversion of this stream into a present value must be tackled in two parts. The present value of £60.50 accruing at end year 1 is £60.50/1·1 = £55 and the present value of £60.50 accruing at the end of year 2 is £60.50/1·21 = £50. The present value of the stream of cost savings is therefore £55+ £50 = £105, which compares favourably with the initial outlay of £100.

Note that the procedure for discounting a two-year stream to a present value effectively involves two questions: (a) what sum will grow in *one* year to £60.50 at a compound rate of 10 per cent? (b) what sum will grow in *two* years to £60.50 at a compound rate of 10 per cent?

6.25   We can now easily see that the present value of a stream of returns of £100 accruing at the end of each of 10 years is given by:

$$PV = \frac{£100}{(1+i)} + \frac{£100}{(1+i)^2} + \frac{£100}{(1+i)^3} + \ldots + \frac{£100}{(1+i)^{10}}$$

Mathematical tables are published to enable present values to be looked up, which is good because the calculation is often finicky. The above formula is sometimes expressed

$$PV = \sum_{k=1}^{10} \frac{R_k}{(1+i)^k}$$

where R_k is the return at the end of year k.

6.26   Recall that we posed the question whether it was worth spending £800 on a machine now if the net yield at the end of each of 10 years was £100, the discount rate being 10 per cent. The present value of the stream of returns is

£91 + £83 + £75 + £68 + £62 + £56 + £51 +
£47 + £42 + £39 = £614,

which is considerably less than the initial outlay required to produce this stream of return. Had the discount rate been 4 per cent instead of 10 per cent, the stream would have had a present value of £810. At 4 per cent, therefore, the venture would have been worth while.

6.27   If the agency is a private firm the reader may be wondering whether the need to discount future returns persists if the firm finances capital expenditures from its own savings or from profits not distributed to shareholders rather than by borrowing. The answer is yes since the firm will have the opportunity of lending funds at 10 per cent or distributing them to shareholders either to lend out on their own account or to put to some preferred use such as consumption. We may summarize by saying that the opportunity cost of funds to the firm is 10 per cent. If a project is not worthwhile at a discount rate of 10 per cent the funds should be put to alternative uses.

6.28 In the foregoing examples we have implied that investment rules for social service agencies and for profit-maximizing firms have in common the need to calculate two time streams—of costs and of benefits—and to compare them by reducing them both to present values at some discount rate. Some readers may find it odd that the rules that apply to profit-maximizing firms should also apply within the social services. In order to throw light on this question we will have to go a little more deeply into reasons why interest rates arise at all. One immediate reason why discount rates should be applied to social service projects is that the investment resources could have been put to some alternative use in the private sector with the result that a public sector project, if it is to prove a worthwhile use of resources, must at least satisfy the same discount rate as the (private sector) project it displaces.

6.29 Perhaps it is best to think of the discount rate as a price like any other price. Just as a wage is the price that must be paid to a worker to divert his labour from other uses and from using his time in his own way, so the interest or discount rate is the price that must be paid to consumers to induce them to postpone the exercise of their claims on present productive capacity, thereby releasing it for use on capital projects, in exchange for a similar claim on future productive capacity. Failure to exercise present claims to consume results in a supply of a certain quantity of loanable funds. If now we talk not in terms of postponing claims on productive capacity but focus attention instead on the supply and demand for loanable funds we can say that the demand for loanable funds at a given discount rate comes from two sources: (i) from private firms and public agencies with capital projects whose net present value is positive at the going discount rate, (ii) from households whose marginal rate of time preference exceeds the going discount rate (if the household is indifferent between £100 now and £114 next year its marginal rate of time preference is said to be 14 per cent and we would expect the household to borrow £100 if it could do so at an interest rate of only 10 per cent). The supply of loanable funds comes from households whose marginal rate of time preference falls short of the rate of discount and from firms with more funds that they can profitably invest internally at the going rate of discount.

6.210 In equilibrium we would expect that these offers and demands for loanable funds would result in the emergence of a single interest or discount rate and in certain closely defined circumstances far removed from today's realities emerge it would. In practice many different rates are to be observed. The question is which is the right one for social service projects? There are two answers. The complicated and difficult answer is that it depends what sort of alternative actually is forgone if the social service project is proceeded with. If a private sector project is displaced then the discount rate might be that used by the private sector in appraising a similar project of its own; if private consumption is displaced then the proper discount rate is the rate of time preference of consumers. In practice there might be difficulties in quantifying the proper rate in each case, to say nothing of the problem of determining what actually is forgone. Those who wish to pursue these questions are directed to the supplementary reading. There is, however, a short and easy answer as to what discount rate public agencies should use: the rate promulgated by the Treasury for that very purpose!

6.3 Discounting—an example

6.31   As an example of the importance of discounting and the discount rate consider the following problem of when to replace a hospital laundry. We will assume there are no complicating factors such as the possibility of contracting out the business and/or replacement with disposables. The present laundry is old; costs are rising. The variable costs per annum of providing 80 tons of laundry is £105,000 in year 1. This is expected to rise by £5,000 each year on account of the increasing age of the equipment and even then only if £5,000, £11,000, and £18,000 worth of additional maintenance work is undertaken in each of three years respectively—in any case the laundry will be completely unserviceable at the end of the three year period. The new laundry is expected to cost £200,000. Variable cost of an annual throughput of 80 tons will be £100,000. With up-to-date equipment this is not expected to rise in the foreseeable future.

6.32   Since the laundry will have to be built anyway, the £200,000 cost will not be saved. However, an important saving is to be made by *postponing* the expenditure and that is the difference between the present value of £200,000 incurred now (i.e. £200,000) and the present value of £200,000 incurred in three years' time [i.e. $£200,000/(1 + i)^3$]. The net benefit from a three-year postponement of the capital outlay is therefore £200,000−£200,000/$(1 + i)^3$. The higher the discount rate, i, the greater is this saving. The choice between these two policies can be summarized in tabular form.

VARIABLE COSTS PER ANNUM OF CONTINUING
WITH EXISTING LAUNDRY AND BUILDING NEW LAUNDRY (£000)

Maintain Old Laundry		Build New Laundry	
At end of year	Extraordinary maintenance outlay	Variable costs	At end of year	Variable costs
1	5	105	1	100
2	11	110	2	100
3	18	115	3	100

If the discount rate is 10 per cent the present (i.e. at the beginning of year 1) value of the cost of operating the old laundry is

$$\frac{110}{(1 + 0 \cdot 1)} + \frac{121}{(1 + 0 \cdot 1)^2} + \frac{133}{(1 + 0 \cdot 1)^3} = \frac{110}{1 \cdot 1} + \frac{121}{1 \cdot 21} + \frac{133}{1 \cdot 331}$$
$$= 100 + 100 + 100 = 300.$$

However, we must deduct from that the saving from the three-year postponement of the new laundry, $200 - 200/1 \cdot 331 = 200 - 150 = 50$. Therefore the present value of operating the old laundry for three years is 250. With the new laundry costs are

$$\frac{100}{1 \cdot 1} + \frac{100}{1 \cdot 21} + \frac{100}{1 \cdot 331} = 91 + 83 + 75 = 249.$$

Plainly, it is just worth incurring the £200,000 expenditure now to effect the saving in variable costs in years 1, 2 and 3. If, however, the discount rate were slightly higher—say 11 per cent—the present value of the cost of operating the old laundry becomes

$$\frac{110}{1 \cdot 11} + \frac{121}{1 \cdot 2321} + \frac{133}{1 \cdot 3676} = 99 + 98 + 97 = 294.$$

Subtract $200 - 200/1.3676 = 54$. The answer is 240. With new laundry costs are:

$$\frac{100}{1 \cdot 11} + \frac{100}{1 \cdot 2321} + \frac{100}{1 \cdot 3676} = 90 + 81 + 73 = 244.$$

At that discount rate a policy of soldiering on with the old laundry just has the edge.

6.33 But we may question whether, even with a 11 per cent discount rate to soldier on for the *entire* three years. If we were to repeat the exercise taking the beginning of year 2 as the present, the calculation becomes:

Old Laundry

$$\frac{121}{1 \cdot 11} + \frac{133}{1 \cdot 2321} - \left(200 - \frac{200}{1 \cdot 2321}\right)$$
$$= \ 109 + 108 - 200 + 162$$
$$= \ 179$$

New Laundry

$$\frac{100}{1 \cdot 11} + \frac{100}{1 \cdot 2321}$$
$$= \ 90 + 81$$
$$= 171$$

It appears that it is worthwhile to postpone the new laundry by only one year.

6.34 When the discount rate is 17 per cent, however, it is worthwhile postponing the new laundry by the full three years.

6.35 This example shows that the discount rate is a crucial variable in determining the time at which to replace a piece of capital equipment. The higher the discount rate the less worth while it becomes to spend now with the objective of saving in the future.

6.4 A word on inflation

6.41 The end of the chapter seems an appropriate point at which to say a word on inflation. In allocative economics we are always comparing the value of one thing with the value of another, e.g. is it worth spending £x m. on a new road to effect time savings of 100,000 vehicle-hours per year? To determine the answer we would attach a money value to time savings in the first year, based on what those who save time are prepared to pay for the savings in appropriate situations. Sometimes, however, the general level of prices rises or falls. If prices are rising by 20 per cent p.a. should we not raise the future value of time savings by this amount? The road then appears a much better investment if there is inflation than if there is not, and the faster the inflation the better it seems. But the alternative output which the £x m. of resources might produce is also rising in nominal value as a result of the inflation. Instead of working out all the possible uses of the £x m. and applying to them a mark-up to represent inflation, it is easier to cancel out the effect of inflation by working in constant prices, normally those of the year in which the project occurs. In short, ignore *general* inflation. However, if some values are expected to fall or rise *relative to the general price level*, allowance should be made for this.

6.5 Summary

6.51 There have been two basic themes in this chapter. The first is that cost must not be assumed to be the same as money expenditure. Cost is about the value of good things forgone, whether these are bought for money or not. The second is that the *timing* of costs and benefits is relevant, and needs to be taken explicitly into account by discounting future streams to equivalent present values. This enables us to reflect accurately the common view that, *other things being equal*, it is better to have good things earlier than later, and bad things later than earlier!

Additional Reading

R. G. Lipsey, *Positive Economics*, Chapter 19, 'The Measurement of Costs' gives a good elementary account of the notion of opportunity cost. E. J. Mishan, *Cost-Benefit Analysis*, Chapter 11, 'Transfer Payments' repays careful reading in that many readers will find it hard to accept that a project which uses otherwise unemployed labour incurs no opportunity cost in doing so even though the going wage is paid. Chapter 12, 'The Use of Shadow Prices', though mainly concerned with constraints on international transactions and inappropriate external values for currencies, should sustain its claim 'to start the reader thinking along the right lines'.

On the techniques of discounting see A. J. Culyer, *The Economics of Social Policy*, Appendix to Chapter 8. The enthused reader is invited to tackle Part IV of Mishan's *Cost-Benefit Analysis*. A comprehensive yet simple treatment of the general topic of investment appraisal is to be found in C. J. Hawkins and D. W. Pearce, *Capital Investment Appraisal*, Macmillan, 1970.

CHAPTER SEVEN

Cost-Benefit Analysis

7.1 Introductory

7.11 The paths trodden in immediately preceding chapters now converge on cost-benefit analysis and its variants. What distinguishes cost-benefit analysis (CBA) from other methods of appraisal is that both costs and benefits are expressed in money terms. This ensures commensurability, the measurement of all quantities against one measuring rod. It is conceivable that in other economies other measuring rods might be found, e.g. cowrie shells, camels, wives, goats. Even in our own economy other measuring rods are possible, even feasible, e.g. in transportation studies the measuring rod might be units of time saved and all costs and benefits could be converted to that. Money, however, has the overwhelming advantage that it is the yardstick against which the largest numer of items of cost and benefit can be measured. This explains why we went to the lengths we did in Chapter Five to show how to attach money values to the benefits produced by social services and why in the following chapter we drew attention to the need to ensure that money costs reflected opportunity costs.

7.12 Instead of a rehearsal of the general principles of cost-benefit analysis, a service adequately provided elsewhere, we shall instead examine CBA in action with a series of blow-by-blow accounts, extracting and emphasizing lessons in commentary.

7.2 Example I

7.21 We choose firstly to examine a water-supply problem, but one that has social service ramifications. In the study we discuss* the

* J. J. Warford and Alan Williams, 'Rural Water Supplies and the Economic of Alternative Location Patterns' in M. G. Kendall, *Cost-Benefit Analysis*, EUP, London, 1971.

authors point out that the policy of providing a mains water supply to all becomes markedly more costly as progressively more remote and sparsely populated areas are reached. The case for mains water as opposed to other sources is the alleged reduction in the risk of water-borne disease. The authors feel unable to quantify or evaluate this reduction in disease risk. Accordingly they accept as a constraint the need for universal provision of mains water and set out to evaluate alternative ways of providing it: take the mains to the people or the people to the mains.

7.22 Of course, this constraint at once removes the study from the pure realm of cost-benefit analysis since one of the principal outputs of the project, reduced health risk, is not valued. Implicitly, of course, it is valued: the value is equal to at least the lowest cost of providing a mains supply to the residents of the area. However it is rare, especially in the area of the social services, to be able to undertake a full CBA. But since the remainder of the study admirably exemplifies the principles of CBA it will repay careful study.

7.23 In discussing the method to be used, the authors explicitly raise some questions of principle:

COSTS AND BENEFITS TO WHOM?

7.24 The answer is to all relevant parties. Valuations of costs and benefits are those of the parties who bear them, whoever they happen to be. Subjective valuations are not always identical with market valuations as will be made apparent when housing is considered. Quite apart from the problem of valuing costs and benefits, there is the problem of what costs and benefits will be changed. In other studies, e.g. of the criminal justice system, a full-blown systems analysis is necessary to answer this question. In this case the categories in which changes would occur could be listed:

Water Supply
Sewage Disposal
Telephones
Postal Services
Electricity
Schools
Housing
Agriculture
Travel to Work
Miscellaneous Transport Effects

Only true opportunity costs are to count. Purely transfer payments such as social security subventions are not to be counted. Since one man's gain is another's loss, for the community as a whole these payments cancel out.

TIME PERIOD AND DISCOUNT RATE

7.25 The first problem was to decide the length of the time period over which costs and benefits would have to be calculated. Since the physical lives of the various pieces of equipment involved was very different, an arbitrary thirty year horizon was chosen. Costs and benefits occurring after this time are unimportant. The present value of £1 accruing thirty years hence is 10p if the discount rate is 8 per cent, 6p if it is 10 per cent. As to the choice of the discount rate itself, the authors presented their results for a range of discount rates to test the sensitivity of the results to that variable.

MARKET PRICES A MEASURE OF OPPORTUNITY COSTS?

7.26 The authors measure the cost of resources by their factor cost, i.e. the money received by the inputs needed to produce them. This involves deducting product taxes from, and adding product subsidies to, market prices. For example, the fuel costs involved in travelling to work include a considerable tax element. In that case the price of fuel overstates the value of the inputs required to produce it and therefore the value of alternative goods the inputs might otherwise have been applied to.

7.27 The three most important items in terms of their contribution to relocation costs were water supply, housing and agriculture. The more interesting points of principle, however, arose within the latter two categories. With these we now deal.

HOUSING

7.28 The net cost of providing mains water etc. to houses in existing sites is given by:
  (a) The cost of installing water mains.
Plus (b) The cost of internal plumbing improvements
Less (c) The increase in the market value of the house due to (a).
Less (d) The increase in the market value of the house due to (b).
The net cost of providing mains water etc. to houses in the new locations is given by:
  (e) The market value of houses on the original site
plus (f) The cost of installing mains water to the new sites
plus (g) The cost of constructing new houses

less (h) The market value of new houses.

Two simplifying assumptions were made:

(i) that the market value of new housing would equal the cost of construction

(ii) that the market value of housing increases by the amount spent on internal plumbing.

7.29 The result of these assumptions is that the differential cost of providing mains water in the present as opposed to the new location is:

(a) The difference in mains installation costs

Plus (b) The market value of the houses in the old locations with mains water.

7.210 Item (b) therefore is the only housing variable left to estimate. The authors suggest that the market value of a house is often less than the householder's subjective valuation, i.e. there is an element of consumer's surplus, since he would not necessarily move without a substantial rise in the price of his own property relative to property values in general.

AGRICULTURE

7.211 Relocation would mean abandonment of those forms of animal husbandry requiring the constant attention of staff. Out would go pigs, poultry and dairy cattle and in would come beef cattle, sheep and crops. In turn this would necessitate some merging of units. Since mains water would not benefit agricultural output if supplied to existing farms, the main task was to calculate the value of output with the existing pattern of agriculture and the value of output with the new arrangements.

7.212 Since agricultural products are subsidized the assessment of net social value involved a removal of subsidy elements from input and output. The cost of hiring a farm manager was taken as a measure of the social opportunity cost of farmers' own services. An interesting special example of valuation problems concerned milk. Though farmers receive a price based on the prices of domestic and industrial uses of milk, weighted in each case by their share of total output, any small change in milk output alters *pari passu* the amount of milk destined for industrial use. Thus valuation of changes in milk output should be valued at the industrial price, which is much lower than the domestic milk price. Given the pervasiveness of subsidy and complex pricing arrangements in farming it would not have been correct to assess changes in farm profitability as a measure of what society as a whole gains or loses from the change.

7.213 We have said before that labour which would otherwise be unemployed has by virtue of that fact alone imposed no opportunity cost in its current use. The post-relocation pattern of agriculture would entail redundancies at least for a time. The wages of the redundant workers were therefore deducted from the cost of pre-relocation agricultural output, suitable assumptions having been made about the time that would elapse before re-employment took place.

7.214 Although we will not repeat the final results of the study, we draw attention to certain of its salient features.

(i) Its ramified nature. Although the object of the project is to eliminate health risk, the main problems were in fact assessment of effects on other social services, notably housing, and even on private industry, mainly farming.

(ii) The extent of modification to market values. How often are valuation problems dealt with by modifying the relevant market price, but also how useful it is to have market prices as a starting point.

7.3 Example II

7.31 The criminal justice system is the domain of the second study we discuss.* The author does not set out to undertake a full cost-benefit analysis but confines himself to a cost-effectiveness analysis of a small part of the system.

7.32 He points out that the chance of the police clearing up a case depends crucially on whether or not they have a named suspect. On the basis of 1,905 crime reports for Los Angeles, the clearance rate for cases with named suspects was found to be 86 per cent while for cases with unnamed suspects the rate was only 12 per cent. The proportion of cases in which there is a named suspect is linked to the probability that a suspect is apprehended at the scene of the crime. This in turn depends upon the length of time that elapses between some individual's decision to report the crime and the arrival of the police on the scene. The exercise is therefore to elucidate the best way of spending money to reduce this time interval. Five alternatives were:

(1) Increase in the number of public call boxes.

(2) Increase in the number of 'complaint clerks' at the police communication centre to reduce queuing delays to incoming calls.

* A. Blumstein, 'Cost Effectiveness Analysis in the Allocation of Police Resources' in M. G. Kendall, *Cost-Benefit Analysis*, EUP, London, 1971.

(3) Installation of a computerized command-and-control system to reduce delays in dispatching cars.

(4) Installation of automatic car locator equipment to identify accurately the car closest to the scene.

(5) Increase in the number of patrol cars to reduce the average distance of the closest available car to the scene.

The comparison is made between the annual cost of an additional unit of the appropriate item of equipment and seconds of delay saved by that unit. The author suggests as a decision rule that money should be spent on a further unit of that item of equipment with the highest number of seconds of delay saved per dollar allocated.

Basic unit added	Annual cost of extra unit $	Seconds of delay saved per $	
Public callbox	50	9·5	
Complaint clerk	35,000	71·7*	0·42†
Command and control system	200,000	119	
Car locator	100,000	47·5	
Patrol car	50,000	21·1	

* *If 2 clerks already allocated*   † *If 3 clerks already allocated*

7.33 It seems that the best way of spending money is to purchase the command and control system. But things are perhaps not as smooth or straightforward as they seem.

(1) Of course since no money value is placed upon the marginal benefits of the system, i.e. ultimately the reduction in crime, we cannot be sure that spending money is worthwhile at all.

(2) If the money value of a second's delay were somehow to be made known we might find that the schedule was downward sloping, i.e. we might have a case of declining marginal benefit. We might find that the dollar value of the 23·8 million seconds saved by the $200,000 command-control system was only $180,000, whereas, quite possibly the 4·75 million seconds saved by the $100,000 car locator equipment were worth $110,000. In that case the better decision would be to buy the car locator equipment despite its lower score in terms of seconds of delay saved per $ of outlay.

(3) Similar problems might be encountered in the schedule of the marginal productivity of the various items of equipment. To take a simple example, if it were decided to spend $400,000 on reducing

response times a second command and control system could hardly be expected to produce the same level of delay savings per $ as the first. Of course, no one is likely to make a mistake like that. But had public callboxes been shown to produce the largest time saving per $ spent, the problem of when or how fast decline set in would have been a real one.

7.4 Example III

The final example is not itself either a cost-benefit or a cost-effectiveness analysis, but it tackles the hardest problem that cost-benefit analysts in this field have to face, with the result that to extend it in the direction of a full CEA would involve problems of a lesser magnitude. The problem* we choose is how to place a money value on the output of a hospital. This involves two stages: (a) deriving a physical measure of the output (b) valuing it.

7.41 A full-blown measure of the effect of hospital treatment on a patient would be the difference between two morbidity streams—the actual morbidity stream between treatment and death and the morbidity stream the patient would experience if no treatment were given. No doubt some suitable discount rate would have to be applied to the stream of benefits. However, the authors do not feel able to consider this more comprehensive approach. Instead they concentrate on the state of the patient on admittance to the hospital and at his first post-discharge out-patient visit.

7.42 The first task, then, is to measure patient's state. The authors argue for a two dimensional characterization—the observable state of the patient's disability and his subjective feelings of distress. In any case both are to be judged by hospital staff. The classification system must be simple enough to be applied quickly and consistently by different assessors and yet it must be fine enough to make useful distinctions. We reproduce it below:

Disability

(1) No disability
(2) Slight social disability

---

* R. M. Rosser and V. C. Watts, 'The Development of a Classification of Morbidity and its Use to Measure the Output of a Hospital and to Analyse the Consistency of the Awards Made by the Courts in Personal Injury Cases', SSRC Conference, 1973.

F

(3) Severe social disability and/or slight impairment of performance at work. Able to do all housework except very heavy tasks.

(4) Choice of work or performance at work severely limited. Housewives and old people able to do light housework only, but able to go out shopping.

(5) Unable to undertake paid employment. Unable to continue any education. Old people confined to home except for escorted outings and short walks and unable to do shopping. Housewives only able to perform a few simple tasks.

(6) Confined to chair or wheelchair or able to move around in the home only with support from an assistant.

(7) Confined to bed.

(8) Unconscious.

Distress

(1) None

(2) Mild

(3) Moderate

(4) Severe

7.43 This classification entails a matrix of 32 possibilities (see p. 73). An intake of patients can be allocated among these states and the matrix of states for these patients noted on their first post-discharge out-patient attendance. A general movement upwards and to the left should be observed if hospital treatment is having positive effects.

7.44 But how are these states to be rendered commensurable? How many of (1,2) are the equivalent of a (8,1)? And what is the relative value of a movement left or upwards at any particular point? And what is its value in money terms? The authors suggest a valuation procedure based on awards of compensation by the courts to victims of injury and disease since 'the aim of these awards is the neutralization of the disability and distress suffered by the plaintiff'. Thus it was possible to develop a scale of the compensation rates the patients would have received if their disabilities had been due to negligence on someone's part. The authors use only the relative values of the various states, the state receiving the lowest award acting as the basic unit or numeraire, i.e. the values assigned to the various states being divided by the value for state (1,2). The result is noted on p. 74.

Distress

	1	2	3	4
1				
2				
3				
4				
5				
6				
7				
8				

Disability

7.45 There seems no good reason why the actual figures should not be used, why only the relativities should count. If that were done, the value of the hospital's output in any given period could be the value of the change in patients' states during the period which could then be compared with the value of output of other regimes. Since the valuation of the costs to be met in effecting this improvement in state is unlikely to present insoluble difficulty, it would be possible to undertake a complete cost-benefit analysis of the hospital's operations and this would be applicable to the health service as a whole.

7.46 While we would not claim the above study as the last word on this problem, we offer it as a good illustration of what can be done if ingenuity is used.

Distress

Disability	1	2	3	4
1	0	1.0	1.9	—
2	2.1	3.0	5.1	8.3
3	4.4	6.5	14	30
4	16	16	31	38
5	52	52	59	66
6	—	59	66	121
7	—	—	114	158
8	123	—	—	—

7.5 Concluding remarks

7.51 Perhaps just one final point should be added to the detailed lessons we have drawn from the illustrations present in this chapter. Although most efforts at project appraisal are not openly intended as CBAS, nevertheless insofar as they recommend courses of action, they implicitly are CBAS. Since this is so, it might be better to recognize this fact and adopt a cost-benefit framework explicitly as a means of lessening the scope for error.

Additional Reading

The best text for a beginner to look at is D. W. Pearce, *Cost-Benefit Analysis*. A good, short introduction is to be found in R. Layard, ed., *Cost-Benefit Analysis*, Penguin, 1972. See the introduction by the editor. Also there are many applications. There is, too, the book we have already had frequent occasion to cite: E. J. Mishan, *Cost-Benefit Analysis*, Allen & Unwin, 1971. There are two interesting collections of papers in addition to Layard: M. G. Kendall, ed., *Cost-Benefit Analysis*, EUP, 1971, and J. N. Wolfe, ed., *Studies in Cost-Benefit and Cost-Effectiveness Analysis*, Allen & Unwin, 1973. Two other collections of studies at a lower level of conceptual difficulty are T. Newton, *Cost-Benefit Analysis in Administration*, Allen & Unwin, 1972, and *Cost-Benefit Analysis in the Public Sector*, IMTA, (now CIPFA). For an advanced treatment of a particular public investment problem in a cost-benefit setting see A. J. Harrison, *The Economics of Transport Appraisal*, Croom Helm Ltd., 1974.

CHAPTER EIGHT

Health and Welfare Services

8.1 Introduction

8.11 Attempts to improve the efficiency of health and welfare services, using the conceptual apparatus set out earlier in this book, have been made both by people with expertise in the 'efficiency' business as such (e.g. Operations Research, Management Consultancy, Organization and Methods, Statisticians, Economists, etc.) and by people actually responsible for operating these services, who have taken the initiative in promoting improvements based on common sense and intuition guided by experience. Unfortunately, the latter type of study is seldom written up in a systematic manner and published, so that comparative evaluation of such work, and the dissemination of successful innovations, depends very much on informal channels of communication. This is a pity, both from the general standpoint of improving the efficiency of these services, and from the particular standpoint of this book, because it implies that such 'local initiatives' are inevitably poorly represented in the material reported here, despite the suspicion that they may well bulk large in the overall volume of relevant work.

8.12 What will be atempted in this chapter is a highly selective survey of published studies, designed to indicate the range rather than the volume of work that has already been done, written up, and reported. The object is to demonstrate the feasibility of applying in a practical manner the various notions of efficiency expounded earlier in this book, and to suggest that there are considerable potential benefits to be gained by doing so, often in rather humdrum and mundane contexts.

8.13 Although health and welfare services have some important peculiarities which distinguish them clearly from other activities, it is important to recognize that much of what they do is common to a

Class No.	Author (surname first)	Date requested 2-16-77
Accession No.	Williams, Alan + Anderson, Robert	
	Title	
No. of copies ordered	Efficiency in the Social Services	
	SBN	List Price
Date ordered	Publisher and Place Martin Robertson + Company Edinburgh University Press, Teviot N.E. 07512	Year 1975
Dealer	Edition or series Volumes	No. of Copies 1 paper $5.00
Date received	Requested by Reginald Olson	Dept. for which Recommended Social Service Bridge
	Reviewed in	
Cost		
L. C. card No.	Approved by	Fund Charged Social Service Bridge

MCL *no*
OF *no*
BIP *ad*
WHIT
BBN
LEV
LC#
 CBI
 BPR
 PW
 NUC
 LJ
 BL
 CH
 WLB
 Date *3/23/77*

wide range of activities. For instance, the choice of the best configuration of laundering facilities for a hospital is not very different
from that for a hotel or for a prison! The best time to replace
vehicles is a problem faced by industry and commerce on a vast
scale as well as by public services. The best place to locate a
'service-point' in relation to its clientele is also a common problem,
as is the best siting of a cluster of facilities each of which depends
on the others for certain services. Another 'standard' problem is
that of determining the best 'capacity' to aim at when the arrival
rate of 'clients' is variable, and yet another concerns the best level
of stocks to hold when excessive stockholding is costly but the
penalties for being caught 'out' are also considerable. There is a
vast literature, especially in the operations research field, on these
problems, and it takes only a little initiative and imagination to
adapt them to fit the health and welfare context.*

8.2 Simple input substitution

8.21 Many suggested improvements in efficiency take the form of
proposals to introduce some new products or materials in place of
those currently being used for some particular purpose. In such
cases the prime intention of innovation is not to vary the nature of
the 'output' or services provided, but to provide that output or
service more cheaply. Whether these potential savings are then used
to expand the service, or to expand some other services, or allowed
to accrue to the community at large in the form of reduced taxes,
etc., is left an open question. It frequently turns out, however, that
apparently minor changes in product use engender quite widespread
repercussions in working methods or in the provision of associated
facilities, so that their appraisal can become extremely complicated
if a comprehensive view of the possible outcomes is sought. It is
typical of all efficiency appraisal that some prior view has to be
taken of the breadth of any study and this needs to be done with due
deliberation, because the conclusions reached will frequently be
very sensitive to the realm of discourse that is pre-selected.

8.22 A typical example of this kind is the one used in a highly

* For a quick review of the possibilities, see, for instance, G. M. Luck,
J. Luckman, B. W. Smith and J. Stringer, *Patients, Hospitals, and Opera-
tional Research*, Tavistock Publications, 1971 (SBN 422 73860 3), and
D. Y. Coomber and A. G. McDonald, 'Operational Research Service' in
Portfolio for Health 2, Oxford Univ. Press (for the Nuffield Provincial
Hospitals Trust) 1973 (SBN 0 19 721377 4).

simplified manner to illustrate what is involved in choosing an appropriate scale of output, namely the decision whether to replace 'reusable' supplies with 'disposable' ones, in the context of a medical/nursing situation. Moreover, because it raises so many problems of principle relevant to a wide range of choices, it is of greater interest than is indicated by its substantive subject matter (pervasive though this itself is). The basic problem is easily stated: would it be cheaper to replace things like sheets, towels, aprons, syringes, etc., which are currently made and bought with the intention of being washed, sterilized and reused, with comparable ones which come in sterile packs, are used once, and thrown away?

8.23 There are, however, several clarificatory questions which need to be posed at the outset. Cheaper to whom? (Are we considering only one particular hospital, or hospitals in general, or the whole NHS, or the whole public sector, or the whole nation?) Cheaper in what terms? (Are we considering only financial savings to the relevant parties or are we including other costs, like time, which may not be reflected in money costs?) Cheaper over what time-space horizon? (Are we considering what the savings might be in the short run, given existing staff skills, equipment, buildings and general layout and support facilities, and taking the present costs of supplies as given, or are we looking further ahead, and envisaging changes in some or all of these things, which may be happening anyway, and/or which might be influenced by the decision under review?) Obviously there is no one definitive answer to these questions; they need to be answered appropriately for each particular decision context, but it is not difficult to imagine that the outcome of the evaluation may well differ markedly from context to context.

8.24 We will consider two actual studies* of this problem, which between them bring out these points quite well. The first study regards the three significant criteria as being 'reduced infection risks; the saving of staff time; and value for money', while the second works explicitly only with costs, though other matters (like staff attitudes, retraining needs, etc.) are discussed. It appeared unlikely, however, that the use of disposables would have a very significant effect on cross infection rates because 'their use alone will neither prevent nor control infections due to other causes such as failure to

* D. K. White, 'Disposables in Hospitals', *The Hospital*, May 1965; and K. N. Armstrong and A. G. Lockett, 'Planning for Disposables', *British Hospital Journal and Social Service Review*, 'Phase 1—Long-term Implications' 8 April 1972, 'Phase 2—Short-term Implications' 15 April 1972, and 'Phase 3—Operational Implications' 22 April 1972.

segregate carriers and infected patients and staff and failure to provide adequate theatres, wards and equipment'. Nevertheless, if properly used, some chances of infection are eliminated by the use of disposables, and so we could expect some small gain.

8.25 The phrase 'if properly used' has wider implications than may appear at first sight, for its raises a fundamental question about the proper basis for the comparisons that have to be made in the evaluation of alternatives. It is well known that these can be done either as 'before/after' studies in particular agencies (i.e. as 'time-series' comparisons) or as 'with/without' studies across a range of agencies at a point in time (i.e. as 'cross-section' comparisons), and the relative advantages and disadvantages of each strategy are pretty obvious. But there is a more subtle strategic element which is often overlooked, namely, should one compare 'ideal' with 'ideal' or 'practical' with 'practical'. To be more specific, should we in this case be comparing what the situation would be if disposables were always used 'according to the book', with what the situation would be if reusables are always treated with scrupulous regard for the rules, even though we know that neither of these situations is realistic? Or should we make due allowance for human frailty and estimate what the actual situation is likely to be in each case with any particular configuration of existing staff, procedures, equipment, buildings, etc.? The former course has the advantage that it provides a standard yardstick from which *ad hoc* adjustments can be made, but the disadvantage that it may lead to exaggerated expectations (and hence subsequent disillusionment) about what may be achieved. This danger is frequently accentuated by the tendency to compare the (imperfect) system already in operation with the (idealized) proposed system, which is obviously a prime recipe for misguided choice and bitter recrimination. On this matter White observes:

> The 'ideal' comparison is obviously between the most efficient procedures involving re-usable items on the one hand and the most efficient procedures involving their disposable counterparts on the other, but the ideal state is elusive. One can only offer the conclusion which a particular hospital has reached, with due reference to all known qualifying factors, and trust to administrative wisdom that such conclusions are not given indiscriminate application.

8.26 If we turn next to the element of staff time, 'the crucial question is whether the savings of time can or should be converted into savings of money'. On this matter it is observed that:

Nursing time saved is particularly difficult to utilise because it is widely disseminated amongst a large number of people and is built up from minutes and seconds saved in various places throughout 24 hours, so that it is not easy to gather together without upsetting established routines and traditional staffing patterns ... Hospitals not in the process of reducing the working hours of nurses might be quite unable to 'collect' the nursing time saved ..., but lost hours of work, unless they were not fully occupied in the first place, which is unlikely, must be made up and money is set aside ... to enable this to be achieved. But it may be better and more economical ... to spend at least part of this extra money on ... products and systems which save nurses' time rather than seek to recruit additional staff, who may be unobtainable anyway.

8.27 There is a wealth of material for analysis here. First, there is the proposition that to save time which cannot then be used is pointless. In practice this is unlikely to manifest itself as strictly 'idle' time, but rather be used for low priority tasks, i.e. tasks of such low value to the system that when time is short they are regarded as not worth doing, or not worth doing so thoroughly. We are therefore saying that such time is of low (or even zero) value to the system, hence it is not worth spending (much) money to get it. In more brutal terms, the value of this time is less than the payment made for it. But, by rearrangement of duties it *is* usually possible *either* to use such time savings more productively within the system, *or* to realize them in the combined form of more leisure time for the staff and less expenditure by the system. In a system with such flexibility, we can assume that the value of the time is accurately reflected in the payment made for it. But time savings will of course be of higher values than this where recruitment difficulties are forcing tasks to be skipped which are regarded as worth hiring staff for, if only they were available at the going rate. Hence the context determines the appropriate money value to place on staff time savings.

8.28 But how staff time savings should be realized (or used) raises issues concerning the appropriate level of performance at which the system should be operating, which go beyond the mere calculation of the most efficient way of operating the system at any pre-selected level of performance. The precise nature of this problem is worth exploring further, because it is deeply embedded (and often confused) in debates of this kind.

Figure 1

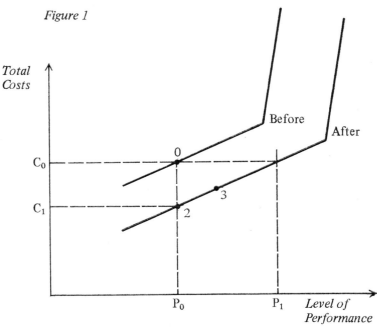

Figure 2

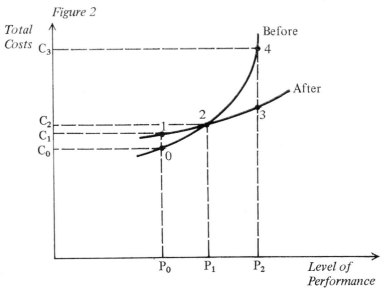

8.29 Even in a fairly clear cut case where disposables are cheaper than reusables at all relevant levels of performance (as in Figure 1, where 'before' means 'with reusables' and 'after' means 'with disposables') there are some tricky problems of interpretation. Suppose the study indicates that at the present level of costs (C_0) the system would perform better (at P_1 instead of P_0) with disposables than with reusables (i.e. position 1 is better than position 0). Suppose that it also shows that at the present level of performance, disposables are cheaper (at C_1 instead of C_0) (i.e. 2 is better than 0). This does not tell us whether 1 is better than 2 or vice versa, or whether we should go for some intermediate position like 3. This requires us to review the optimum level of performance in the light of the new cost situation, i.e. requires us to value marginal benefits as well as marginal costs, so it is a much more broad ranging exercise which cannot be resolved by cost comparisons alone.

8.210 If we turn to the more complex situation depicted in Figure 2 we are in still deeper water, because there disposables are only cheaper at higher levels of performance, being more expensive at lower levels. We then face possibilities such as the following: at the current levels of performance (P_0) disposables are more expensive (at C_1 rather than C_0) hence position 0 is better than position 1. But if we envisage raising levels of performance beyond P_1 (where, at 2, both systems have the same costs, C_2), say to P_2, it may be extremely costly to achieve such performance levels with reusables (at 4), but much cheaper to do so (at 3) with disposables. Hence the choice of system is intrinsically bound up with the choice of performance level.

8.211 This is a good opportunity to bring out one of the difficulties encountered in this study, where it was observed that 'disposables, although generally representing higher standards, cost more (at least initially) by comparison with traditional techniques'. Put more crudely in terms comparable to Figures 1 and 2, the study established two points such as B (before) and A (after) in Figure 3. But in principle we could convert this into a Figure 1 type situation with either disposables or reusables coming out uniformly better (see Figures 4a and 4b respectively), and we cannot even rule out a complex situation of a Figure 2 kind. In Figure 5a is presented a case where B is the most efficient system at the present level and A at the higher level, but unfortunately we cannot rule out the possibility depicted in Figure 5b where both A and B are the *wrong* systems for their respective performance levels!

8.212 Thus the conclusion to be drawn here is that *without further information* about the costs of the respective systems at other per-

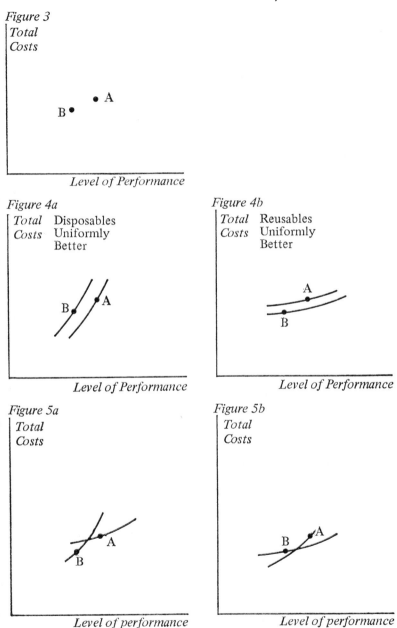

Figure 3
Total Costs
B• •A
Level of Performance

Figure 4a
Total Costs Disposables Uniformly Better
B A
Level of Performance

Figure 4b
Total Costs Reusables Uniformly Better
A B
Level of Performance

Figure 5a
Total Costs
B A
Level of performance

Figure 5b
Total Costs
B A
Level of performance

formance levels we can draw no policy conclusions whatever from the information contained in Figure 3 (and hence from studies which essentially do the same thing).

8.213 Problems of scale economies were dealt with as follows in White's study: For disposables, the purchase 'costs quoted . . . are those incurred by independent and small-scale buying. In general it may be suggested that a scaling down . . . by approximately 8 per cent would give a fair indication of the cost when large-scale buying and contracting can be introduced'. For laundering costs 'a very rough estimate of £500 per annum notionally saved' was arrived at 'by applying the then average cost of 3·16d per article laundered at the Central . . . group laundry . . . However this theoretical saving has not been brought to account . . . chiefly because of the extreme difficulties experienced and anticipated in making the savings real. For one thing the scale of activity is too small in relation to the total . . .' so that 'the continuing costs of the laundry have remained . . . virtually unaffected . . . Secondly, the average cost' is calculated over 'a wide range of items of which the "real" cost of laundering may be anything from a penny to a shilling'. 'Finally, it is clear that there is an optimum throughput . . . to which machinery, fuel consumption and labour use is carefully geared, so that the only result of introducing laundry-saving disposables in unfavourable circumstances will be to leave the laundry working below capacity without any real savings.'

8.214 Clearly there is an analogy here with the earlier discussion on the saving of staff time, as well as to the discussion in Chapter Three on estimating laundry costs. In essence the problems arise from starting with average costs; the failure to distinguish fixed from variables costs at an early stage leads to the convoluted arguments which follow. The simple proposition is that it is marginal costs which must be estimated and used in this situation, with 'costs' carefully valued to reflect the value of the resources released (if any). As regards the optimum configuration of facilities, this of course becomes more malleable through time as major components of it become due for replacement.

8.215 This aspect is brought out more clearly in the second study, which concentrates much more explicitly on timing and uncertainty, and on the selection of a strategy for both the short run and the long run. Here the essential point is the time-related context of costs, although volume-related aspects are still important. For example:

As disposables become cheaper than the cost of laundering

durables . . . they will clearly replace laundry processes. However, parts of the new systems appropriate for disposables will have to be introduced before they are fully utilised, while the utilisation of laundering facilities will also be falling . . . Here is the crunch . . ., directly the disposable is introduced the overall operating costs may increase. The trick is . . . to programme the contraction of laundering operations and introduce to fill the demand gap thus created . . . before falling disposable prices actually meet rising laundering costs . . .

8.216 What is needed here is a systematic comparison of short and long term costs, because we face a situation in which it is being argued that some increase in short term costs should be accepted for the sake of the long term gains. It is a pity that discounting was not explicitly introduced (it is argued that 'this operation has been omitted . . . for simplicity and at any realistic rate the ranking of alternatives remains unchanged anyway') since it crucially affects the *timing* decision.

The higher the discount rate, the less acceptable are increased present costs for the sake of lower future ones, so the less acceptable will be expensive capital schemes designed to replace existing systems with high running costs. Since existing facilities tend to get costlier as they get older, a high discount rate therefore delays (but does not rule out) the switch over (as we saw earlier in Chapter Six).

8.217 One final aspect of this problem which is worth noting is the range of costs that are considered. Disposables involve higher costs of 'disposal', which may, of course, not fall on the hospital but on the local authority or some other agency. Similar considerations apply to 'contract laundering', and although from a hospital's point of view the price paid is the 'cost', the price paid may nevertheless be higher than the true (marginal) cost for the community, since the price will include an element to cover overheads, etc., the inclusion of which, as we have seen, exaggerates potential costs (and cost-savings) in the short run.

8.3 Place of treatment

8.31 The preceding study showed that even if you start with simple switches of materials you are likely to be led to consider associated changes over a much wider realm of activity, and this tends to be true wherever you start. In this section we are going to look at what happens if the analysis is initiated in a different way, by asking where should treatment take place (interpreting 'treatment' very broadly)? We can follow the analysis through in much the same way, though less fully here since many of the relevant points will now be obvious from the foregoing discussion.

8.32 One of the commonest situations in the personal social services is that in which the professional (GP, midwife, social worker) has to meet the client (for an examination, or to administer some treatment, or to impart information). A fundamental question is 'where and when should the meeting take place?' The 'where' will depend on the relative mobility of the two parties (there may, of course, be more than two), the likely need for associated facilities, whether the meeting is more likely to be productive in one place than another. The 'when' will depend on the urgency of the meeting (i.e. the cost of delay), or more generally whether the timing influences the effectiveness of the meeting, and the availability of parties (i.e. the competing claims upon their time).

8.33 The choices usually resolve themselves into three strategic possibilities: the client stays in his own home and all meetings occur there; the client remains based in his own home but meetings occur elsewhere; the client is transferred from his own home to an institution of some kind, and meetings take place there. This strategic division is probably the most fundamental influence on working methods and the kind of facilities that are provided, and deserves to be considered (and reconsidered from time to time) with great care.

8.34 There are many fields in which these problems arise, and here we will consider only one of them, the care of the elderly. Here there are a wide range of services involved, some centred on simple domiciliary support (home helps, meals on wheels), some on total institutional care (long-stay geriatric wards of hospitals, residential homes for the elderly) with intermediate agencies such as day centres and hospital out-patient departments, and some (like GPs) contributing at all points in the spectrum. In addition, a generalized role is played by social workers and welfare agencies of one kind or another, by neighbours and by relatives and friends. It is an enormous problem area, in both magnitude and complexity, and no one study can hope to do it justice, but we will use as an example*

---

* R. Wager, *Care of the Elderly* (an exercise in cost-benefit analysis commissioned by Essex County Council), published by the Institute of Municipal Treasurers and Accountants, London, March 1972.

one which covers a fair amount of territory, and hence conveys very well the essential flavour of an 'efficiency' calculus in this field.

8.35 The object of the study was to estimate the relative merits of domiciliary and institutional care for the elderly within one particular authority, Essex. The detailed results obtained are, therefore, strictly speaking specific to that authority. The study tackles four broad questions:

(a) Are domiciliary care and residential care really feasible alternatives for the elderly?
(b) Is it possible to assess the state of the potential clientele in a fairly objective way that will be useful for operational purposes?
(c) Is it possible to establish a suitable basis for comparing the costs of such widely differing facilities as domiciliary care and residential homes?
(d) Is it possible to identify patterns of care that are likely to be less costly without being less effective?

To each of these questions a guardedly affirmative answer is given, and we will consider in more detail below how each question was tackled.

8.36 With respect to (a) a survey was conducted which found that there is a range of moderate incapacity to which either domiciliary care or residential care would be an appropriate response.

[The view] that there is no satisfactory alternative to residential care for old people applying for admission to welfare homes . . . is apparently based on the assumption that the sole attribute of those applying . . . is severe incapacity. However, the survey found that, in addition to incapacity, such other factors as accommodation problems, difficulties with household relationships and loneliness were important in giving rise to nearly half the applications . . . Indeed the index of incapacity showed that 28 per cent of applicants experience slight or no incapacity and a further 23 per cent could be described moderately incapacitated.

8.37 The 'index of incapacity' just mentioned is the way in which the study answers question (b). It is built up by rating clients according to 14 different 'components', which turn out to 'cluster' into five groups as follows:

G

(I) Sensory perceptions: Defective sight; defective hearing
(II) Intellectual processes: Difficulties with speech communication; mental confusion and instability
(III) Personal Care: Difficulty dressing; difficulty washing; incontinence
(IV) Physical mobility and absence of stability: Falls and giddiness; mobility indoors; mobility outdoors; bathing; negotiating stairs and steps
(V) Domestic duties: House cleaning; meal preparation

In building up the index scores of 0, 1 or 2 are assigned to each of the 14 components according to whether the applicant coped 'with little or no difficulty', 'with moderate difficulty' or 'with considerable difficulty or not at all'. The overall scores were then grouped as follows:

Score	Percentage of population surveyed falling in each group
Score 0 = No incapacity	4
Scores 1 to 5 = Slight incapacity	24
Scores 6 to 8 = Moderate incapacity	23
Scores 9 to 15 = Substantial incapacity	37
Score 16 and over = Severe incapacity	12

8.38 This is a characteristic way of dealing with the *valuation* of client states without explicitly using the term 'value', yet it does imply relative valuation. In this case a client whose vision worsened from moderate to severe incapacity would be held to have been 'compensated' if continence improved from 'moderate' to 'little or no' difficulty, since each changes the rating by one point. There are, in fact, 28 one-point differences each of which is equally valued in the index scoring. Where one operates with the incapacity grouping rather than the incapacity scores, things become still more tricky because only changes that cause clients to cross the boundaries between groups will be 'valued', all others, within the 'threshold' being ignored (i.e. having zero values). Since the incapacity groupings are not themselves assigned explicit weights, the valuations associated with them are left vague, and hence liable to differing interpretations (i.e. implicit valuations) by different people.

8.39 When we turn to question (c), concerning the appropriate basis for cost comparisons, the study eschews the usual financial basis of local authority expenditures alone, and embarks on the much more ambitious task of calculating real resource costs to the community at large. In pursuing this task it is noted that

the continued occupation of owner-occupied housing is included as a resource cost of domiciliary care, even though the owner pays no rent. Conversely, taxes have been excluded as far as possible; they are more of the nature of 'transfer payments' rather than resource costs since they do not represent direct payments for the consumption of specific quantities of goods and services.

8.310 Moreover, since it is relative expansion or contraction of existing services that is under consideration 'the appropriate costs . . . are the marginal costs of services'. Unfortunately, however, 'these have been approximated by calculating average costs per unit, after excluding expenditure on central administration. Other administrative expenditure, however, which is an integral part of a particular service, such as the cost of home help organizers, and is more likely to vary directly with the level of output, has been included.' This is likely to overstate the costs of small changes in activity levels, unless the services are operating at such high pressure that marginal costs are above average costs, due, for instance, to the payment of overtime rates or corresponding special remuneration for accepting unusually large workloads.

8.311 Finally, any expenditure in the current accounts relating to the finance of capital expenditure is excluded as the cost of capital schemes is included specifically. As an incidental feature of this part of the exercise a calculation was made of the comparative costs of residential homes of different sizes which indicated that construction costs per place varied as shown in the table on page 90.*

It will be seen that it costs about £330 per place more in 50-place than in 60-place homes, and another £350 more per place in 40-place homes, which raises acutely problems such as

(1) is the quality of care better in small homes than in large ones? (and, if an affirmative answer is given, how is this measured?).

(2) is it so much better as to justify the extra outlay? (for instance, if one had an 'index of care' which increased from 100 to 120 as one

---

* In what follows, complications over actual occupancy rates, and differential running costs have been ignored. It can be verified from the original study that these considerations do not affect the conclusions drawn below.

| £ *Costs* | | *Size of home* | |
per place	40 places	50 places	60 places
Land	350	280	230
Construction and Design	2625	2344	2064
Furniture and Equipment	197	197	197
Total	3172	2821	2491

NB All figures here (and later in this section) are at 1969/70 prices

switched from 60 place homes to 50 place homes, but only from 120 to 125 if one switched from 50 place homes to 40 place homes, would you consider both switches worthwhile, only the former, or neither, and how?).

(3) if the quality of care is better in smaller homes than in large ones, there remains the problem of whether to spend one's budget (of say £100,000) providing about 31 high quality places or 40 lower quality ones, in other words the choice transforms itself into one of weighing the value of the extra benefit accruing to the fortunate 31 against the 9 who will be excluded altogether.

8.312 This brings us to the stage where we can confront question (d), i.e. whether it is possible to identify patterns of care that are likely to be less costly without being less effective. A direct confrontation with this question would require a sensitive operational measure of the effectiveness of different modes of care, which was not available. So instead the problem is tackled in a more roundabout way, relying heavily on the professional judgements of welfare workers as to what 'packages' of support services were likely to be effective, and then costing these out. These were then compared with the cost margins generated by alternative types of accommodation, to see how the overall picture shaped up.

8.313 The outcome of the overall cost comparison in the Essex Study was as shown in the table on the opposite page. It will be noted that, apart from the detached three bedroom house, the variation over the range 5 per cent to 10 per cent in the discount rate used to convert capital costs into equivalent current costs does not affect the rank ordering of the alternatives. This may be

COMBINED CAPITAL AND DAY-TO-DAY COSTS OF RESIDENTIAL AND
DOMICILIARY CARE ON A WEEKLY BASIS (EXCLUDING DOMICILIARY
SERVICES)

Type of accommodation	*Average resource costs per person per week*	
	Using 10 per cent discount rate £	Using 5 per cent discount rate £
Residential accommodation (40 places)	17.00	14.00
Old people living in normal housing		
Higher value, e.g. detached 3-bedroom house	19.50	13.50
Medium value, e.g. semi-det 3-bedroom house	15.50	11.00
Lower value, e.g. semi-det 2-bedroom house	13.00	10.00
Old people living in normal housing with others	5.50 to 7.00	5.00 to 6.00
Old peoples flatlets with warden (single person) or attached to residential home	13.50 to 14.00	11.00 to 11.50

interpreted as indicating that old people occupying higher valued
properties impose more costs on the community than housing them
in residential homes, unless discount rates of about 5 per cent or less
are appropriate.

8.314 The costs of domiciliary support services (with the excep-
tion of supervision by a warden in the case of sheltered accommodation) were excluded from the above figures, so that they have to be
interpreted with care. As the report says:

> The figures . . . indicate the economic saving to the community
> through making small purpose-built dwellings available to elderly
> people 'underoccupying' larger dwellings which have become too
> big for their needs. The benefit to the community's housing prob-
> lem arises irrespective of whether the accommodation released is

local authority or privately owned; this suggests that the optimum use of the community's housing resources is not served by the practice . . . whereby some local housing authorities do not consider applications for accommodation from owner-occupiers . . .

Although the needs of some applicants were solely related to the provision of more suitable accommodation, in most cases domiciliary services were required and their cost must be added to the cost . . . set out in the table. Living in sheltered housing and lower value 'normal' housing will only tend to use less resources than residential care if the cost of domiciliary services for the occupants is below a level of about £3 or £4 per week. As an illustration, £3 will 'buy' . . . five meals-on-wheels and seven hours of home help. About half of the programmes of care recommended by the social welfare officers for applicants they felt could continue in the community would have cost less than £3 per week, and about three quarters less than £4.

For higher value accommodation the basic cost differential is smaller or reversed and intensive domiciliary care in such cases may well be significantly costlier in resource terms than residential accommodation. This finding illustrates the difference in approach of cost-benefit analysis and financial appraisal. If the County Council's costs alone were considered, high levels of domiciliary care would normally be justified before the costs approached that of residential care, but such a policy would in fact pre-empt a greater share of the community's resources when viewed in a wider sense.

The greatest scope for intensive domiciliary care at lower cost than residential care is clearly in those cases where elderly people are living with others, when the basic cost differential is in the region of £8 to £10 per week, depending on the rate of discount applied.

8.315 There are clearly many other features of this problem which could be pursued, and on which work has been and is being done. The use of voluntary workers and friends and neighbours raises interesting problems about costs (what is their leisure sacrifice worth, and if they are in scarce supply, how should they be distributed to best effect . . . assuming they have alternative uses!) The costs to relatives of supporting people who need a great deal of attention can be very costly in emotional as well as in physical terms, and highly disruptive of normal family relationships and activities. These costs too need to be considered in estimating the relative merits of institutional and domiciliary care. The Essex study indicated that it is the 'living with relatives case' that offers the greatest scope for providing domiciliary support before overall costs reach those of residential care, and this suggests that one way to approach the problem might be by offering that much help and seeing whether it would ease the stress and strain sufficiently to keep that mode of care viable for a longer period than at present.

8.316 What this study indicates (with others of its ilk) is that even where direct valuation of output is ruled out for one reason or another, a really sophisticated analysis of the costs of a fair range of alternatives can shed very useful light in certain strategic choices facing policy-makers. It does not, of course, make their choices for them but enables them to make their judgements in a better informed and systematic framework than is all too frequently the case.

8.4 The evaluation of alternative treatments

8.41 To a considerable extent the choice of *place* of treatment turned out to involve differences in the *mode* of treatment, so again we found ourselves drawn more deeply into the problem than appeared necessary at first sight. Here we are going to start with some specific medical conditions and consider alternative therapies, but we shall again find ourselves drawn into wider considerations, of the kind encountered earlier.

8.42 One of the simplest instances is the substitution of one drug for another, and an interesting case from our point of view is contained in a report* of an investigation into the time savings to be generated by replacing, wherever possible, addictive pain killing drugs subject to Dangerous Drugs Legislation (DDAS) with non-dangerous analgesics with a comparable action (non-DDAS). The study does not, however, concentrate on the costs of the respective drugs themselves, but rather on the hidden costs of the safety precautions associated with dangerous drugs.

8.43 The additional costs of DDAS over non-DDAS arise mainly because the time spent administering a DDA was on average five times as great as that spent on a non-DDA (about $7\frac{1}{2}$ minutes compared with $1\frac{1}{2}$ minutes). In addition there are big differences in the time spent dispensing DDAS compared with non-DDAS, but since

* A. J. Culyer and A. K. Maynard, 'The Costs of Dangerous Drugs Legislation in England and Wales', *Medical Care*, Vol. 8, No. 6 (1970).

most drugs are dispensed in the daily ward order this is not a large element. Other costs include the costs of the stationery used in the paperwork associated with the extra records to be kept for DDAS, regulation enforcement costs, disposal of waste, security measures in the pharmacy and in receipt and handling of consignments, and the cost of retaining records for inspection later if required. Each of these adds a little, but not much, to the staff costs, which are the major item.

8.44 If we calculate time cost savings per annum for a hospital of 300 beds, then

Assuming that half the patients received on average one dose per day, and that the typical nurse works a 50 hour week, the additional time is about 100 nurse-weeks per year. In terms of expenditure, the additional costs ... may be estimated at approximately £1627 assuming that a State Registered Nurse (salary £942 per annum) and a nurse of age over 25 (salary £630 per annum) both administer DDAS and attend to patients in the drug round [1970 figures]

This clearly raises all the questions considered earlier (in section 2 of this chapter) concerning the conditions under which it is proper to value time savings in this way. On this the authors observe

Clearly it is not meaningful to interpret a saving of £500 per annum ... as the opportunity to buy the services of ·833 nurses (at £600) a year. Even nurses do not come in such handy packages! [But it is possible] to dispense with the equivalent of ·833 nurses in ... any particular job. Thus, the saving ... could be effected ... when some medical inputs are substituted for others.

8.45 The authors also re-examine the assumption

that current wages and salaries paid to staff represent their true (marginal) value to society and, furthermore, that the possible changes are also marginal. The existence of a current shortage of nursing services indicates, for example, that a shadow price higher than the current wage ought to be used, and if the change is not marginal, the *future* (true) marginal value should be used plus one half the difference between that and the *current* (true) marginal value as an approximation for the correct shadow price under discrete changes. In the case considered here, only the former problem causes us any concern, but since we have not been able to discover by how much to adjust the present data ... the calculations presented above are, in our view, minimal ...

Thus the argument is not only that these time savings are valuable (i.e. they can be *used*, and will not just result in idle time, in which case they would be valueless) but that nurses' time is more valuable than its market price indicates (this is the meaning of the reference to a high 'shadow' price), hence the figures shown are likely to underestimate the time savings.

8.46 In order to see how sensitive these estimates are to variations in the assumed level of dosage and in the staff used, the following table is presented:

ESTIMATED ADDITIONAL COSTS OF DANGEROUS DRUGS
REGULATIONS £P.A.

Staff used		*Doses per patient day*				
for DDA	for non-DDA	$\frac{1}{8}$	$\frac{1}{4}$	$\frac{1}{3}$	$\frac{1}{2}$	$\frac{2}{3}$
Sister and SRN	SRN and Nurse	586	1172	1562	2344	3125
Sister and SRN	Sister and SRN	545	1090	1454	2180	2907
SRN and Nurse	SRN and Nurse	407	814	1085	1627	2170

As well as enabling us to test whether particular assumptions made in the face of uncertainty are critical to the outcome, this serves also as a useful ready-reckoner whereby others could work out, for their own situation the staff costs likely to accrue to them, given their particular pattern of activities.

8.47 A further point that is worth abstracting from this study is the authors' observation that

The consequent freeing of resources which this implied could provide the opportunity to tackle the problems of post-operative pain. For example, the availability of non-DDA analgesics could release nurse hours which could then be utilized to institute a pain round and give pain relief when needed. Another point ... is that if a non-DDA substitute of comparable price existed, substantial economies in hospital procedures might be achieved regardless of the hospital uses found for resources thus released ...

Again, the choice between these possible uses of economized resources is a policy choice including benefit valuations and not just a
technical matter for those calculating relative costs.

    8.48 Let us now turn to a similar case, also involving two alter-
native treatments, but which also involves a comparison of inpatient
and outpatient status, namely, the treatment for varicose veins.*
Basically the alternatives are surgery or injection-compression
sclerotherapy. The former involves an average length of stay in hospital of 4·1 days for men and 3·5 days for women, ranging from 2
to 15 days. Afterwards patients come to an outpatient clinic, at
which men made a mean of 2·1 and women 2·3 attendances. The
other treatment, by elastic stockings and injections at an outpatient
clinic, involves the patient in walking at least three miles a day and
coming back to hospital if the leg becomes painful. The patient was
usually seen at the clinic after a week and any varicosities which
were still patent were injected and the leg rebandaged. Compression
was maintained by bandages for six weeks after the last injection,
and the patient was seen at the clinic until these were discarded. The
average number of clinic attendances for each leg was 7·1 for men
and 7·4 for women. In the medical follow up over three years 'the
two groups have been found to resemble each other in every respect
except that of treatment'. Since the 'choice should be the one that
leads to as good clinical results as any other and should be the most
economical of manpower, money and resources,' it therefore looks
like a straight cost-comparison.

    8.49 The costs are considered in two groups, cost to the health
service, and costs to the patient. 'For neither form of treatment was
it feasible to estimate the capital cost of the facilities utilised so that
the estimates of cost only relate to running cost.' This obviously
implies that the results obtained refer essentially to adjustments in
the pattern of activity small enough in scale not to require redeploy-
ment of major facilities (like the provision of operating theatres or
hospital beds). The effect of this limitation to running costs only is
likely to be to understate the costs of surgery relative to those of
injection-compression sclerotherapy.

    8.410 Looking first at the costs to the health service, they were
built up in the following manner:

    The salaries for each of the staff taking part in a typical clinic
    were assessed. The cleaning, building maintenance and heating

* D. Piachaud and J. M. Weddell, 'The Economics of Treating Varicose
Veins', *International Journal of Epidemiology* (1972).

were all included. The secretarial costs covered the costs of medical records. The average cost of an outpatient session was £41.50. The average number of patients treated per session was 31; the average number of clinic attendances per patient was 7.3. Thus the average total cost per patient of outpatient injection-compression treatment was £9.77 [All figures are in 1967/8 prices.]

It will be noted that the 'average' referred to here is average *variable* costs, and averaged across the range of cases stated.

8.411 Estimating the costs to the health service of surgical treatment is a much tougher proposition:

The construction *ab initio* of a complete system to cost the surgical treatment of varicose veins would, if it were to cover the full range of hospital costs, be a vast undertaking.

Existing information is, however, quite adequate to estimate most of the costs. The . . . Hospital Costing return . . . provides average costs per inpatient week for each of a number of categories of expenditure and unit costs for most of the major departments.

A number of categories of expenditure may be assumed to be 'shared' equally by all inpatients . . . Domestic Staff, Catering, Staff Residence, Laundry, Power, Light and Heat, Building and Engineering Maintenance, General Administration, General Portering, General Cleaning, Maintenance of Grounds, Transport, Other Services . . . , Equipment. The inclusion of this last category —equipment—needs some explanation; while certain items of equipment may rarely or never be used on varicose vein patients, it is virtually impossible to say . . . [which] are essential and . . . [which] . . . are not, given the countless contingencies for which a hospital must be prepared. Further, the use of an operating theatre for varicose vein surgery precludes its use for other types of surgery and therefore any equipment primarily for these . . . must necessarily lie idle.

The sum of these 'shared costs' was £29.09 per inpatient week or £15.38 for the average varicose vein patients' stay of 3.7 days.

The cost of nursing and medical staff cannot be assumed to be shared equally by all patients.

On the basis of a small survey it was estimated that one-quarter of all nursing time was spent on 'general' activities . . . , time spent on particular nursing activities associated with varicose vein patients averaged 1½ hours during the inpatient stay; in addition approximately half an hour was required for outpatient attendances subsequent to discharge . . . making a total nursing cost of £2.02 per patient.

A similar method was used to estimate medical staff costs . . . of £2.01 per patient.

The average cost per operation for the use of operating theatre (drugs, dressings, equipment and staff employed on theatre duties, etc.) was £13.71 . . . [and] . . . is a reasonable approximation to the cost of varicose vein operations.

Pathology tests, X rays, and drugs were specially recorded and amount in all to £8.23 per patient. Medical record costs were taken to be the average per case, viz. £2.76, giving a total of £44.22 for the hospital costs of surgery for varicose veins.

8.412 The essential costs to patients were based on a follow-up survey which revealed that:

The mean number of days taken off work at the time of treatment and for convalescence was 6·4 days for those treated by injection-compression, and 31·3 days for those treated surgically.

The average loss of earnings of those in full time employment receiving surgical treatment was £118 and of those receiving injection-compression treatment was £29.

All those admitted to hospital had a spell of convalescence, while only 11 of the 38 in full time employment who were treated by injection-compression sclerotherapy took any time off at all . . . Hospital admission seems to correlate directly with the demand for and apparent need of convalescence whereas outpatient treatment, which probably gives rise to as much or more discomfort does not.

This highlights the weakness that patients' time is valued only if it would otherwise have been used to produce goods and services (i.e. leisure time has *no* value!) However, this omission, like others, merely understates the relative costs of surgery, and a fuller analysis would only reinforce the conclusion, which is 'that injection-compression treatment involves substantially lower costs to the community than surgical treatment'.

Additional Reading

Apart from the references cited earlier in this chapter, and the material on output measurement cited at the end of Chapter Four, those with an interest in exploring further the cost-benefit approach to health and welfare services might like to consult the following survey articles:

Alan Williams, 'The Cost-Benefit Approach', *British Medical Bulletin*, Vol. 30, No. 3 (1974).

Herbert E. Klarman, 'Application of Cost-Benefit Analysis to the Health Services and the Special Case of Technological Innovation', *International Journal of Health Services*, Vol. 4, No. 2, 1974, which also contains an extensive bibliography.

Both of these are written for non-economists and are quite accessible.

For those willing to venture off the nursery slopes and swallow some rather larger draughts of economists' jargon, the following may be recommended (in ascending order of difficulty):

M. M. Hauser, ed., *The Economics of Medical Care*, Allen & Unwin, 1972.

Mark Perlman, ed., *The Economics of Health and Medical Care*, Macmillan, 1974.

M. H. Cooper and A. J. Culyer, eds., *Health Economics*, Penguin Education, 1973.

The first of these is a collection of studies investigating various aspects of the health care system, primarily relating to British experience, but with contributions on Swedish, French and US experience. The second is a sizeable volume covering a wide range of issues facing primarily the US and European health services, varying in style and approach from the broad historical sweep to detailed econometric analysis of particular aspects. The third volume is a book of readings encompassing what have become standard references in the field of health economics among economists themselves. They are not excessively technical, however, and give a good (and cheap!) introduction to the important problems in this field as perceived by those writing in it.

CHAPTER NINE

The Provision of Outdoor Recreation Facilities

9.1 The nature of the market

9.11 In this chapter we show how to draw on the principles of earlier chapters to appraise investment opportunities in recreation facilities. We want to develop the means to decide the extent of facilities to be provided, where to provide them and when.

9.12 First of all we will have to spend a little time examining the special features of the supply of and the demand for outdoor recreation. At first sight the problem of investment in recreation facilities might seem a straightforward set of problems akin to deciding on investment in capacity to produce other sorts of goods. For example, replace 'recreation' by 'electricity generation' and do we not have a precisely analogous problem? Would it not be better to direct the reader to one of the excellent manuals available on the appraisal of power station investment and ask him to substitute 'recreation' whenever the words 'electricity' and 'power' are encountered?

9.13 An important distinction between electricity and recreation is that the latter is frequently provided either free or at a charge greatly below what would be needed to cover total costs of provision. Two reasons can be advanced to explain why this is so:

(a) Recreation is often looked upon as a merit good, that is, society or the electorate think it a good, wholesome thing for people in general to engage in outdoor recreation.

(b) A common feature of the supply of recreation facilities is that it costs no more to admit 500 people to their use than it does to admit 50 or five. Any charge might drive away consumers with a positive marginal valuation while making no offsetting cost saving. In short, marginal cost is often zero.

The fact of free provision raises problems of efficient level of provision: how much of the free good should be provided, where and when?

9.14 In sharp contrast to standard paradigms of goods, outdoor recreation is immobile. It cannot be transported to the customer. The important consequence is that, unlike electricity the market for which is national so that even large additions to capacity account for but a small share of the market, a recreation site has a market bounded by the distance people are willing to travel in order to reach it. A new recreation site might account for a very large proportion of the relevant market. The corresponding situation for a transportable good at national level would be the introduction of a completely new good.

9.15 These two features, free provision and significant share of the relevant market go a long way to explain why the methods of appraisal presented in this chapter are necessary. However, two subsidiary features of recreation provision also deserve mention:

(1) Recreation is often only one of many goods and services jointly produced by a project. To exemplify, a system of dams in a river might bring forth the following benefits; (i) flood control (ii) hydro-electricity generation (iii) storage of water in the rainy season for use in the dry season (iv) water-based recreation (v) fish-farming. It is comparatively rare for a project to be pronounced worthwhile by virtue of its recreation benefits alone. Only if the sum of benefits from all uses exceeds the costs of the project and the losses which it causes, e.g. loss of agricultural output from flooded land, will the project be undertaken.

(2) Responsibility for managing recreation facilities and for providing them frequently devolves on some public body. This suggests that the interests of society as a whole should count.

9.2 A measure of value

9.21 The nub of our problem is to elicit consumers' valuation of a free good. Let us imagine that a completely new good is to be supplied free of charge to as many people as would like to consume it. Let us also suppose that we know the consumers' aggregate marginal valuation curve for this good telling us how much of the good would be bought at each of a set of prices were prices to be charged.

9.22 From each unit the consumers gain their MV less what they

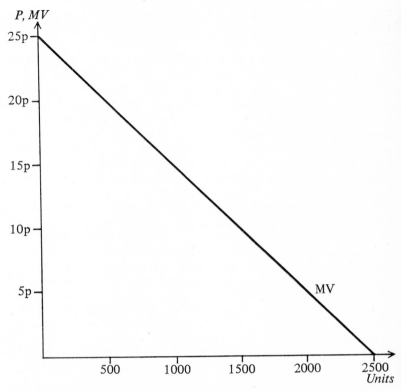

have to pay for it. For the first unit of the good consumers would be willing to pay 25p but are actually charged nothing. They therefore gain a surplus of 25p through being offered the first unit free of charge. By parity of reasoning surplus gained on the 501st unit is 20p, on the 2001st unit is 5p, until eventually the 2500th unit produces a surplus of zero, consumers being sated with the good at that level of consumption. By summing the gain on each unit of the good from the 1st to the 2500th it is easy to see that the value of the total gain to consumers is represented by the total area under the MV curve. Since the MV schedule is a straight line and therefore, together with the axes, encloses a right-angled triangle, the total value represented by the area is $\frac{1}{2} \times 2500 \times 25p = £312.50$. Consumers therefore value the opportunity to consume the good free of charge at £312.50 per month or week, whichever is the period of time to which the MV schedule relates. This is a measure of the consumers' surplus, the total of what consumers would be prepared to pay for the opportunity to consume the good at a given price less what they actually are called upon to pay.

9.3 How to value an existing facility

9.31 Two difficulties must be overcome before we are able to use this analysis to appraise proposals for new recreation sites:

(a) The derivation of the MV curve for a single existing recreation site,

and, since our purpose is to provide information of use in investment decisions,

(b) The derivation of the MV curve for a recreation site that does not yet exist.

9.32 As we have already tackled (a) in Chapter Five on the money valuation of benefits when we were appraising a change in the siting of a town's library, we offer only a brief recapitulation here. In order to build up an MV schedule for an existing site we must observe the number of trips that take place at each of a range of prices. The price paid for a recreation trip to a site is not, or not only, the money price charged at the entrance to the site. It is the value of what trippers must sacrifice in order to gain access to the site and this will be made up of the trippers' travel costs, e.g. petrol, wear and tear, oil, etc., and the value of the opportunity the trippers forgo by using their time to undertake the trip in question rather than using it any other way. Apart from any entry fee, the sacrifice made by trippers is related to distance.

9.33 The next problem is to observe how trip numbers vary as distance from the site varies. If a single site is being considered it is useful to divide up the site's catchment area into rings concentric on the site itself. Every visitor originating within a given ring can then reasonably be assumed to pay the same 'distance-price', based on the average distance-price ring-dwellers would have to pay. However, there might be two reasons why the number of trips varies between rings: the distance-prices vary—this is the variable whose influence we wish to isolate—or the population differs between rings. To eliminate the effects of population variation therefore we express trips generated in terms of trips per thousand zone population. Now it will be possible to observe the variation of trips per 1,000 population as the distance-price varies. Add the entry fee if any to the distance-price to get the total price of a trip and we are in a position to derive a marginal

H

valuation schedule. The actual curve is usually fitted to the data by simple statistical techniques. There is of course the problem of how to establish the money value of travel time and also of how to assess accurately the vehicle-related costs of travel. But since these problems have been tackled in closely related contexts by government departments we urge that the values arrived at there be shamelessly poached for the present purpose.

9.34 If the catchment area comprises seven zones successively ten pence 'further away' from the site, we might obtain the following MV curve:

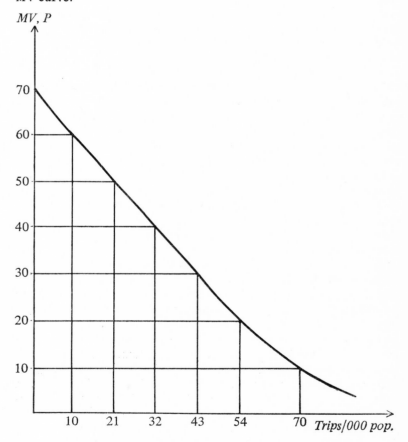

Total consumers' surplus is given by the area under the curve and above the zonal price, multiplied by the number of thousands in each zone, and summed over all zones. If there were only one thousand inhabitants in each zone we would be able to set down the area which represented total surplus as shown on page 106.

9.35 There is an alternative way of calculating surplus, though the answer would be the same. The method is to build up an MV curve for the site by making hypothetical changes in the entry fee. If there are 1000 people in each zone, we know from the previous but one diagram that at price 0, visit rate would be $70+54+43+32+21+10=230$. If prices were raised to 10p the number of visitors from each zone could be found by raising the zonal travel price by 10p and reading off the number of trips generated, in this case $54+43+32+21+10=160$. And so on for entry prices of 20p, 30p etc. The consumers' surplus would be given by the total area under this curve, assuming that in fact no charge for admission was levied. This method can boast no advantage over the method previously outlined.

9.36 In the interests of greater accuracy, however, complications are often introduced into the basic relationship between number of trips and price. It is important to recognize that zones may not be homogeneous with respect to certain variables which may, together with price, influence the number of trips generated per 000 population, e.g. the level of income per head, car ownership, family circumstances. If these variables were felt to be important, they could be included with price in a multivariate regression. In essence this means that we would have a separately identifiable MV schedule for each level of income or whatever the variable happens to be. The principles of surplus calculation remain unaltered. For a given zone, surplus is the area above the actual price for that zone under whichever MV curve is appropriate to the characteristics of that zone. However, if variables other than price are to be considered, it is often desirable to organize zones other than in concentric bands— often local authority subdivisions will be appropriate. In any case it is best to ensure that zones are selected so that variations within zones is as small as possible.

9.4 How to value a proposed facility

9.41 The procedure so far applies only to facilities that already exist. How do we go about deriving the surplus consumers would gain from facilities that do not yet exist? The only way to proceed is by comparison with facilities that do exist. If the prospective facility closely resembles some existing facility in the type of

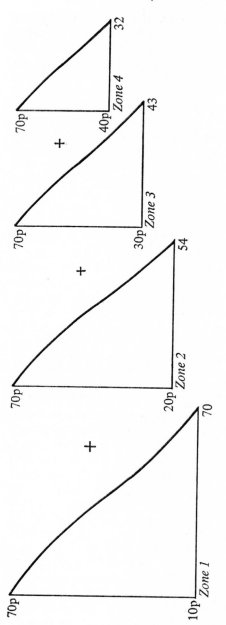

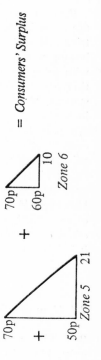

= *Consumers' Surplus*

recreation it will provide, then we derive an MV schedule for the existing facility in the manner outlined above and apply it to the proposed site in the following manner. If the catchment areas for the two sites clearly do not overlap, e.g. if the existing facility is situated in Northumberland and the proposed facility in Cornwall, we can apply the MV curve to the new site, the only changes being in the populations of the zones and their socio-economic characteristics. This would mean of course that only by chance would the same social valuation be placed on the new facility as on the old, despite the fact that the same basic relationship is assumed. The much more common situation where the new facility is to be sited within the catchment area of the existing facility we have already dealt with in Chapter Five when we discussed the issue of public library siting. We will, however, briefly recapitulate. For each zone calculate the price of both the existing and the proposed facility. Using the MV curve for the existing facility calculate the consumers' surplus which would accrue from each facility if it were the only one. If the consumers' surplus to be derived from the new facility exceeds that from the existing facility, the gain in consumers' surplus from having the new facility is the *difference* in consumers' surplus for the two facilities. The social valuation of the new site is this figure summed over all zones.

9.42 However, it is much more usual to find that the proposed new facility cannot be said exactly to resemble any facility already existing. This lack of homogeneity may be due to differences in the mix of facilities offered at the new site, for example, if a new facility offered power-boating and water-skiing but no fishing or bathing and had little to commend it in the way of general sightseeing, it might be best to seek out sites at which power-boating and water-skiing did take place and try to develop an MV schedule not for the existing site as a whole but for these two particular activities at the existing site. Then calculate separately the consumers' surplus from each activity at the new site and sum to find the social valuation of the new site. Possibly different existing sites could be used to derive the MV curves for the two activities.

9.43 An alternative way of dealing with the problem of the partial homogeneity of a new site with an old is to proceed as Mansfield did in his calculation of the social valuation of the recreation potential of the Morecambe Bay Barrage.* In some ways this was

* N. W. Mansfield, 'The Estimation of Benefits Accruing from the Construction of a Major Recreation Facility' in *Cost-Benefit Analysis in the Public Sector*, IMTA Conference, 1971.

a unique recreational opportunity in that there was no other estuary barrage in the UK. However, its proximity to, indeed contiguity with, the Lake District suggested that it would play the role of relieving recreation pressure on the Lakes. But Mansfield recognized that the new site did not have the unique qualities popularly associated with the Lake District. To deal with this problem he devised the notion of qualified homogeneity, which enabled him to use the MV curve for the Lake District whilst avoiding the necessity to make the rather extreme assumption of complete homogeneity.

   9.44 Mansfield's method was this. Suppose for a given zone the prices of the Lakes and of the Bay were P_L and P_B respectively and that P_B was less than P_L. All trips which would not have taken place in the absence of the Bay, T_LT_A, would go to the Bay and would be

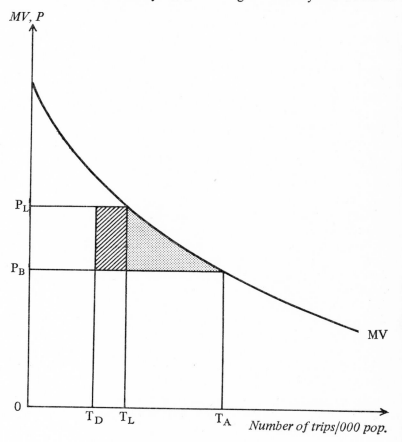

credited with the full surplus from generated trips as represented by the stippled triangle, just as if the Bay were completely homogeneous with the Lakes. Of trips that would have been made to the Lakes in pre-Bay days (OT_L), however, and this is where qualified homogeneity comes in, it was assumed, despite the Bay's relative cheapness, that not all would divert. The proportion which would divert was related to the *difference* between the two prices in such a way that the larger the disparity in price, i.e. the lower P_B relative to P_L, the greater the proportion of trips to divert. Specifically, the proportion to divert was assumed to be $(P_L - P_B)/\frac{1}{2}(P_L + P_B)$. In the diagram $T_D T_L$ trips divert to the Bay, the surplus to diverters being $T_D T_L \times (P_L - P_B)$, or the shaded area. Total consumers' surplus produced by the Bay is the shaded area plus the stippled area summed over all zones for which the price for the Bay was less than the price for the Lakes. No surplus accrued to the populations of zones for which the price of the Lakes was the lower, as no trips from there were assumed to divert to the Bay.

9.45 This is perhaps an opportune moment at which to pause and related the foregoing to cost-benefit analysis. We have talked a lot about the social valuation of the recreational potential of a site and we have identified this with consumers' surplus. How would we extend the analysis to a full-blown CBA? On the benefit side we have consumers' surplus accruing over the particular time period to which the MV curve relates, whatever it happens to be, say a year. The same exercise would have to be repeated for each of the years of the project's life as there is no reason to assume that consumer's surplus will be the same in every year. Indeed, there is every reason to believe it will be different. Population, car ownership and incomes are expected to rise. The behaviour of the distance-price depends on the balance of the rising value of time (due to rising incomes) and the behaviour of vehicle-related costs, of which the direction of change is less certain. For a fuller discussion of these issues the reader is directed to Mansfield's study. At any rate, having determined the consumers' surplus for each of the years of the life of the project, the next thing to do is to bring this stream of benefits to a present value by applying a discount rate in the way outlined in Chapter Six. Do the same to the other benefits of the project and to the costs. Hence a decision can be reached about the worthwhileness of the project.

9.46 A plea is often made that cost-benefit analysis should incorporate distributional weightings, that is, that benefits should be marked up or down recording some index of the prosperity of the beneficiaries of the project. It is not for analysts to intrude their views as to what values these weights should take. That is a question for the client or decision-maker. However, it is for analysts to make sure that it will be possible to identify beneficiaries by income group should distributional weighting be thought desirable. Often this is not an easy task. Happily, however, it is less difficult in the present context than in most. In fact, we already provided for this possibility when we recommended the following form for the trip generation function, which we now formally state:

$$T_{ij} = f(C_{ij}, Y_i, Z_i)$$

the number of trips from zone i to facility j, T_{ij}, is a function of the distance price from the zone i to the facility j, C_{ij}, an income index for zone i, Y_i, and other potentially important variables Z_i. If we hold Y_i and Z_i constant we are left with a function which relates number of trips to distance price—i.e. the MV curve—for those particular values of Y_i and Z_i. It is therefore possible to associate every slice of consumers' surplus with a particular income level. The decision-maker can then, if he likes, say, 'Multiply the consumers' surplus attributable to the poorest zones by 2, and that of those from the richest zones by half. This operation would have more important consequences if the overall purpose of the exercise were to *choose* between sites, since then it would be possible to favour a site from which poorer people would benefit more than the better off, while also giving weight to the intrinsic quality and accessibility of the two sites, which is the particular strength of the whole approach. As an additional refinement, if income data could be gleaned which related to those actually making the trips, that would be preferable to applying an average income for a zone to all who came from that zone.

9.47 This point is more or less as far as the bulk of the work on recreation economics has reached, except that little attention has hitherto been paid to distributional questions. It could be argued that we have not come very far. Now, however, is the time to peer into the crystal ball.

9.5 Towards a strategy for investment

9.51 The analytical apparatus we have explored so far really applies to a situation where one new recreational site is to be appraised. It is better, however, at choosing one from a number of alternative sites. The reason the analysis has developed in this way is that problems have arisen in this way. Alternative reservoir programmes are put forward by the water supply authorities and economists are brought in at a late stage to advise on the social valuation of recreation for each alternative. Rarely are economists asked to advise on the location, number and timing of facilities. But the time will come when economists are asked to develop future strategies for recreational investment as such. How will these problems be tackled?

9.52 The first task is to explain the present pattern of recreational trip-making in the area in question. In order to make the problem manageable it will be necessary to divide recreational trips into fairly obvious categories, e.g. visiting the beach, visiting historic houses, country parks, etc. Having split the demand for trips into self-contained categories the problem is to formulate a hypothesis to explain the level of trips made from each zone to each site. Three sets of explanatory variables are likely to prove to have influence on the dependent variable:

(a) Origin-related characteristics—level of car-ownership, income, family circumstances, etc.

(b) Site-related characteristics—the attractiveness of the site relative to others

(c) Prices, including distance-price and entry fee of the site itself and of all competing sites.

9.53 The need to include some index of the attractiveness of the sites is unfortunate since it entails incorporating 'the expert's' subjective judgements and these are notoriously difficult to replicate in a reliable way. The need to include the prices of competing sites is important in this case not because the prices of sites are expected to fluctuate over time relative to each other, but because inhabitants of different zones face not only different prices for a given site but also different prices for competing sites. The reason for this in turn is that prices are related to distance.

The precise form of this function would be dictated by the results of a statistical exercise. The social valuation of any given site, i.e. consumers' surplus, would be derived in much the same way as before.

9.54 There are two ways in which the above schema could be used in an investment strategy.

(1) Supposing that as time passed the MV curves for particular sites moved outward in response to the growing prosperity of recreationists. It is possible that the physical capacity of any one site might be reached with the result that at the going entry free demand exceeded supply. Though there is no need to suppose that entry fee would rise in response, it is true that a greater sacrifice of time in the

form queuing would be exacted. The total price, including now the queuing-time-price, would therefore rise. But the new price would represent a change in one of the variables affecting the generation of trips and their distribution among competing sites. An equilibrium congestion penalty can be produced using an iterative process in the following way. If excess demand is encountered at a site add a small congestion penalty to the price of that site and enter the new site price into every equation in which it appears. This will produce a fresh set of trips for each site. Continue until the excess demand is choked off. The resulting congestion penalty will be an indication of consumers' marginal valuation of a small addition to capacity at the site and can be compared with the cost of the addition to see if an addition is worthwhile. If additions to capacity can be made only in discrete lumps, such as of size AB in the diagram on the opposite page, the appropriate increase in surplus produced by AB (the shaded area) would have to be offset against the cost of providing AB.

(2) But even if there is no question of congestion at any site it is nevertheless possible that it might be worthwhile building a new site, although the social valuation of the new site would have to be taken as that of an existing site in a different, and by implication superior, location. The basic method is to take each facility, move it hypothetically to all possible sites at which a facility of that kind could be located and calculate surplus for the new site. The social valuation of the new facility would be that of the new site minus its cost. Choose the kind of facility and the location which maximizes this figure. Of course the amount of calculation involved would be enormous but should prove manageable by use of computers.

9.55 This method would also be appropriate even if there were already congestion at some site and it might show that it would be better to open up a new facility rather than to expand some existing one.

9.56 These proposals for recreational investment appraisal in a multisite system must be regarded as prospective and suggestive and not received and well-established dogma. They constitute what the authors see in the mind's eye while peering into the crystal ball.

9.6 Some pitfalls to avoid

9.61 Finally, the reader should be warned that is easy to be seduced into thinking that other methods of appraising investment

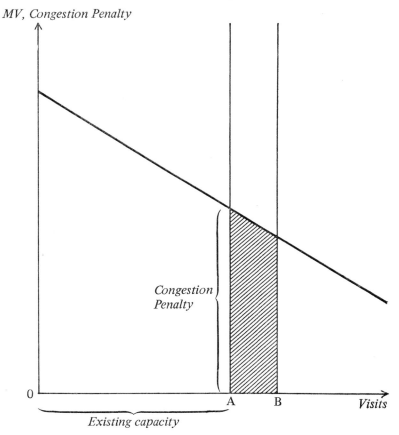

MV, Congestion Penalty

Congestion
Penalty

0

A   B   Visits

Existing capacity

in recreation facilities are simpler and better that what we have proposed, and easier to understand. While we concede them their greater simplicity and comprehensibility, we nevertheless deny their superiority and indeed their usefulness.

9.62 First of all, it has been suggested that the worth, in some undefined sense, of a recreation facility is the amount of money people actually do spend to use it (heresy number one). We, it will be recalled, emphasized that the social valuation of the facility was the amount people were prepared to pay minus what they were actually called upon to pay (where 'pay' is construed as 'give up' and involves the value of non-monetary as well as monetary sacrifice). If the following diagram is an MV curve for a site and OP_A is the distance-price from zone A,

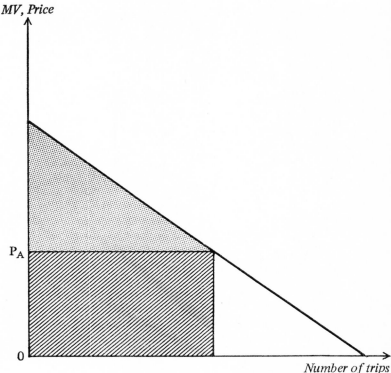

our measure of social valuation is the stippled triangle; that implied by heresy number one is the shaded rectangle.

By the assumptions of consumer behaviour theory, however, the shaded rectangle is not the value of the recreation trips, but the value of the extra goods and services consumers would purchase were the recreation site no longer available. But since consumers do freely choose to spend the amount represented by the shaded rectangle on recreation trips rather than on other goods and services it is a reasonable supposition that they gain extra satisfaction from doing so; the measure of this is consumers' surplus.

9.63 Heresy number two is a variant of heresy number one. It is claimed that the value of recreation at a site is the value of what people must give up to get there plus anything they may happen to spend en route, e.g. on having meals, beer, purchasing souvenirs. Since the actual expediture approach was dismissed as wrong, it is difficult to claim that the present suggestion is wronger. It is, however, no better. Clearly expenditure en route is not a measure of what trip-makers *have* to give up to reach the site. It is expenditure on wholly different goods and expenditure, moreover, that might well have been made however the trip-makers had chosen to spend that day. It is irrelevant to their valuation of a particular recreation site.

9.64 Thirdly, the claim is occasionally heard that the choice between two recreation sites should be made on the basis of the number of visitors each is likely to attract. If the MV curves for the two sites are different, then the crude numbers criterion is unlikely to be a good one.

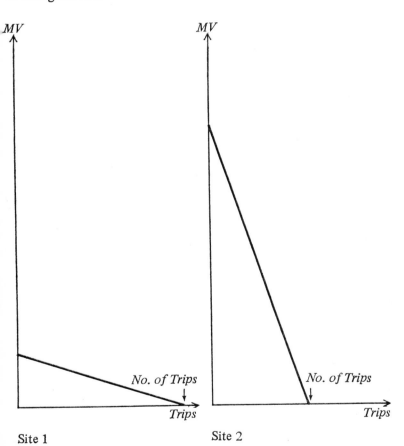

Site 1   Site 2

Although Site 1 attracts more custom than Site 2, it is plain that those attracted to Site 2 value their trips more highly than those attracted to Site 1, and to an extent that swamps the difference in numbers. Even if the intrinsic attractiveness of the two sites were the same, different MV curves for the sites themselves might be found, since their accessibility might be different. In any cases, however many visitors are expected at a site, that does not warrant its construction, since it is not clear that the benefits exceed the costs.

9.65 The reader should be aware that these heresies are not usually expressed as baldly as they are here. Frequently they are cunningly disguised and often appear very persuasive. The art lies in detecting them. But if the reader masters the consumers' surplus approach to the social valuation of recreation sites he should be able not only to avoid heresies himself but detach others from them.

Additional Reading

For a good review of actual studies in recreation economics consult J. G. Gibson, 'Recreation Cost-Benefit Analysis: a Review of English Case Studies', *Planning Outlook*, Summer 1974. See also his references. Those who have assimilated the contents of Chapter Nine might think how to transform into something more useful the article by A. J. Veal ('Estimating Demand at Urban Recreation Facilities') in the same issue of the same periodical. Does Veal not come close to perpetrating heresy number three? Another interesting article is K. D. Goldin, 'Recreation Parks and Beaches: Peak Demand, Quality and Management', *Journal of Leisure Research*, Vol. III, No. 2, 1971.

CHAPTER TEN

Efficient Provision
of Police Protection

10.1 Some features of Cost-Benefit Analysis

10.11 It will be our aim in this chapter to show how to apply cost-benefit analysis to the police service, although we shall by no means be able to say the final word on the subject. In order to remind the reader what is involved in CBA, a few general scene-setting remarks, chosen with the particular example of law in mind, are in order.

10.12 The object of a CBA is to find out whether some project, loosely defined, constitutes a more worthwhile use of society's resources than any alternative to which these resources might be put. CBA springs most readily to mind in the context of large projects requiring substantial initial outlays to secure benefits over a number of years, e.g. a third airport for London, a fixed Channel link, motorways, underground railways. However, there is no reason why CBA cannot be used to appraise non-capital projects such as changes in operating practice.

10.13 The essence of the approach is this: if the benefits of x exceed the costs of x, do x; if not, do not do x. Costs and benefits must be measured in the same units otherwise they cannot meaningfully be compared to arrive at a decision. The unit is, in the overwhelming number of cases, money, since that is the yardstick against which the largest number of items can most readily be measured.

10.14 The reference group is society *as a whole*. This means that we must count the costs and benefits of a project no matter to whom they accrue. Of course this raises difficulties. Often gainers and losers are hard to identify and their participation in the project as gainers or losers is not the result of their own freely made choice, e.g., those exposed to noise from a new airport or motorway. Their valuations must be elicited and counted in as costs or benefits of the project as the case may be. But we must be careful to leave out of account payments which are merely transfers of purchasing power from one member or set of members of society to another, e.g. if a road-building project in N.E. England uses labour that would otherwise be unemployed a saving of £y in unemployment benefit will result. But that does not mean £y is a benefit of the project. It means that a different set of people now exercise command over £y of goods and services, so that society as a whole is neither better nor worse off as a result of £y changing pockets.

10.15 The consequences of some of these seemingly innocuous statements turn out to be rather surprising in the context of crime and punishment, as the reader may already have worked out for himself.

10.16 Finally, the costs and benefits used in CBA are to receive the values those actually involved would place upon them. In practice this means that we usually try to find circumstances in which the individual freely chooses to exchange money for the good in question. An example will make this point clearer. If additional noise is to be inflicted on the residents of a certain area we might try to assess the value those involved might place on the noise if there were some market in which they could buy a lowered decibel level, by the device of looking at the differences in house prices in noisy as opposed to quiet locations elsewhere in the country, and add in any differential value of sales of noise-reducing equipment such as double-glazing, ear plugs, etc., that is observed in the two 'control' areas. (We use the expression 'control' areas because we are trying to perform an experiment akin to a controlled experiment in the physical sciences, varying the magnitude of one feature of the environment whilst holding the others constant.) There is one qualification to the general principle of giving costs and benefits the subjective values of those involved: the decision-maker may take the view that costs and benefits accruing to low-income persons have a greater significance for society's welfare than those accruing to high-income persons. That is, the decision-maker might want to apply a distributional value-judgement.

10.2 CBA and police service

10.21 We now turn from general issues to the particular example of the police service. Let us deal with easy questions first. The inputs of manpower and machinery employed in the police service are already couched in money terms. Both labour and equipment must be purchased in markets. We can therefore take outlays on these items as measuring of the value of the opportunity forgone in putting them to this rather than some other use.

10.22 It is when we come to think of the *outputs* of the police service that problems arise. In general we may assert that the chief output of the service is prevention of offences, although it must be noted in passing that the police perform other useful functions such as reducing traffic congestion, expediting the functioning of other emergency services, rounding up stray animals, finding lost children, giving directions to tourists and not forgetting, of course, their traditional role as an unfailing source of the correct time. The police can prevent offences in two main ways:

(i) directly: deterring offences by maintaining a high probability that offenders will be caught,

(ii) indirectly: reducing future crimes by apprehending offenders and thus ensuring their passage through correctional agencies, e.g. prison, probation.

It is at once plain that we cannot look upon a police division as a self-contained operation, for the prevention of crime by apprehension of offenders depends upon the contribution of the courts and correctional agencies, and costs are incurred by these agencies in producing the end result. Moreover, the efficiency of these agencies downstream of the police constitutes an important determinant of the efficiency of the resources used by the police service itself. If the correction process were wholly ineffective in changing the subsequent careers of convicted offenders, and in addition failed to deter others, there would be little point in having the police detect and apprehend, though it must be acknowledged that custodial sentences might lessen society's exposure to habitual offenders. The upshot is that in order to decide the division of police effort in the directions identified above as 'direct' and 'indirect', it is necessary to consider the costs and benefits of the criminal justice system as a whole. To this we now turn.

10.3 The criminal justice system as a whole

10.31 Leaving aside for the moment the question of placing a value on prevented offences, we will concentrate on how to value the costs incurred 'downstream' of the police in order to secure them.

I

Furthermore, we will take as given the efficiency with which the downsteam agencies achieve good results, though that issue invites fascinating exploration. Suppose an offender is tried and given a custodial sentence. What are the costs to society, remembering that the offender is himself part of society?

10.32 The resources used by the courts constitute buildings, judges and court officials, police officers, counsel, jurors, witnesses. Given that we can take the salaries or fees per hour of judges, counsel (whether legal aid is granted or not), officials and the police as true social costs without need of adjustment, two problems remain:

(a) How to allocate the costs of buildings and their maintenance to cases

(b) How to deal with the costs of jurors and witnesses.

(a) The problem is the distinction between average and marginal costs. It is tempting to say that the cost per case is the total cost of the depreciation on the building plus heating, cleaning, etc. divided by the number of cases. At we have said before in other contexts, that could be a misleading measure of the opportunities forgone. If the prospective change in the number of cases were small probably no extra cost would be incurred/saved by a few more/less cases, i.e. marginal cost might be low while average cost is high. But if, for example, a few more cases necessitate construction of a new court-house, the marginal cost could be quite high, though average cost might change comparatively little. The question would have to be decided in the light of prevailing circumstances.

(b) The costs incurred by society through the courts' claim on the time of jurors and witnesses form a good example of costs that are not met by the agency that imposes them. The costs would be principally the value of the time forgone by these people plus, less importantly, differences from everyday values in the cost of fares and meals. The value of time forgone might be the value of output lost through absence from work and that is to be measured using the relevant wage-rate. Deduct any costs and the value of inconvenience involved in work and add in the inconvenience involved in attendance at court. These probably cancel out. The monetary compensation made to jurors and witnesses is irrelevant as is the issue whether they are paid as normal or not.

10.33 Just as it has been argued that a volunteer army imposes lower costs on society than a conscripted army, so it has been argued that a voluntary, paid system of recruiting jurors would be preferable to the present system of conscription qualified by exemption, on the grounds that, assuming that potential jurors can be arranged in ascending order of the inconvenience they attach to jury service, conscription takes a cross-section while a voluntary, paid arrangement takes those from the lower echelons of the rank order. We will content ourselves with just a mention of this possibility.

10.34 However, the social costs of custody in prison are probably much greater than costs at the trial stage. The valuation of costs of buildings and staff presents no special difficulty. The problems arise with prisoner-related costs. These might be estimated as

+ Value of prisoners' 'outside' output
− Value of 'outside' consumption
− Value of 'inside' output
+ Value of means of subsistence 'inside'

Such an estimate, however, implicitly assigns a zero weight to the losses prisoners incur through being denied the opportunity freely to make decisions about what to produce and what to consume. In the light of what we said about prisoners being counted as members of society, is this right? A measure of this loss that might appeal to some economists is the bribe that would be necessary to induce the prisoners to volunteer to serve the sentences imposed upon them, there being, however, no presumption that it should actually be paid. On the other hand, it can be argued that it is correct to omit this item since offenders voluntarily assume the risks of capture and that the subjective value of the risks of capture are already reflected in the rewards they derive from offending.

10.35 Lastly, a minor issue. As a result of the imprisonment of an offender it is possible that his dependants now become a charge on the state for their subsistence. This should not be counted as a cost to society since it is merely a transfer of purchasing power from one set of people (taxpayers) to another set (offenders' dependants).

10.36 Readers might care to note, though no doubt they have already done so, how frequently we have (a) counted as social costs items that are not paid for out of public funds (b) failed to count as social costs items that are paid for out of public funds. Let us repeat the principle that social costs are not to be identified with calls on the public purse, though of course calls on the public purse in many instances do measure social cost.

10.4 Valuing the output of the system

10.41 We have spent much time discussing proper measures of costs of crime prevention. Now is the time to consider how to value the system's output, which we have provisionally identified as prevented crime.

10.42 What is it worth to society to prevent an offence? At the outset we must recognize that the analysis that applies to one set of offences will not necessarily apply to others. For example, we shall be concentrating on property offences, chiefly theft, but what we say will not apply without qualification to crimes against the person, about which we shall say a little, still less to 'crimes without victims', like prostitution, about which we shall say nothing.

10.43 Theft is the crime *prima facie* most susceptible of economic analysis. In evaluating losses from theft we are at once faced with the problem that since one party's loss is the other's gain, theft is a mere transfer involving no net loss to society as a whole. The implication of this view is that the police ought not to waste time trying to prevent theft but should concentrate on other, socially harmful offences. If, however, the decision-maker reacts against this approach and assigns a zero welfare significance to offenders' gains from theft then the social cost of the transfer is the subjective value to the victim of what is stolen. The market value of what is stolen might be a reasonable measure of this loss.

10.44 However, it is not necessary to invoke this *deus ex machina* to demonstrate that theft imposes social costs. It has been pointed out by Tullock that theft belongs to an important class of transaction which we can call 'contested transfers': it is because the potential parties to the transaction put resources into contesting the transfer that social costs arise. In the standard case of goods and services both parties come together because of a mutual coincidence of wants: the shopkeeper has a supply of goods and a demand for cash and the customer has a demand for goods and a supply of cash. Since they do business voluntarily, both must be better off as a result of the transaction. There is therefore no reason for the police to prevent people from going to the shops. The shopkeeper gains to the tune of his profit margin, which can be looked upon as the supply price of his services, and the customer gains to the extent that the arrangement enables him to improve his welfare by exchanging his labour for goods produced by others rather than engaging in direct subsistence activity. In contrast, where theft is concerned, the potential offender's desire to effect the transfer is opposed by the potential victim's desire to prevent it. Both have an incentive to commit resources to prevent the success of the other party.

10.45 In order to see what use can be made of this important feature of contested transactions let us examine the approach of Shoup and Mehay, who carried out a CBA of certain aspects of police patrol in California. One element of the social loss from theft, they argue, is the alternative legitimate income forgone by the offender. However, they say, since 'as some observers have pointed, there is a strong empirical relationship between low income and the propensity to commit property crimes . . . it may be that the thief's alternative earnings are below those he can earn in crime'. This leads them to conclude that the amount stolen would overstate the offender's forgone legitimate earnings and therefore his opportunity costs. However, this is to ignore certain elements of the opportunity costs of earning the higher illicit income: the risks of capture and punishment must be offset against the additional monetary return from illicit activity.

10.46 Perhaps it is possible to justify in the following way a rule of thumb that the amount stolen does provide an estimate of offenders' opportunity costs. If we assume offenders to act so as to maximize their satisfaction it follows that they will continue to steal until £1 stolen is just offset by the subjective value of the inputs (including risk of undergoing punishment, time, capital equipment etc.) they must devote to stealing it.

10.47 What has not been noticed, however, is that much the same argument holds on the victims' side. Potential victims can prevent theft in a variety of ways, e.g. by (a) expenditure on locks, bolts and shutters, (b) employment of security staff and dogs, (c) location of factory or dwelling at places which in the absence of theft risk would be less preferred, (d) changes in asset-holding patterns induced by risk of loss through theft, (e) use of time for leisure rather than for producing what is liable to be stolen. If the potential victim seeks to maximize his satisfaction he will pursue theft-prevention measures up to the point at which £1's opportunity forgone (whether this represents actual expenditure as in (a) and (b) or subjective valuation of theft-induced changes as in (c), (d) and (e)) will just forestall the loss of £1 (in expected value terms) through theft.

10.48 While these issues undoubtedly require analysis at a more sophisticated level, the simple analysis offered here appears to justify a rule of thumb that the prevention of a theft is worth up to twice what is stolen. If a zero welfare significance is assigned to offenders' gains then the social loss from theft is worth up to *three times* the amount stolen. But it is noteworthy that even without this it is possible to demonstrate that theft is unequivocably a social evil.

10.49 When it comes to placing a money value on the non-monetary aspects of crime such as injury and death, Shoup and Mehay borrow from the well-established stamping grounds of 'boneyard economics' such as health and road accidents. They consider two main categories of loss: (a) loss of earnings through hospitalization or the termination of life (b) costs of hospital treatment. It is fortunate that in both cases standard figures are in use for road accidents in the state in which the study is set. The adoption of these figures for valuing the relevant outputs of crime prevention will serve to ensure a proper allocation of resources among the various means of preventing injury and loss of life, e.g. road safety measures, health service investment, crime prevention etc. Whether the values used in these fields are conceptually well-based is an issue that cannot be pursued here.

THE SHOUP–MEHAY VALUATIONS

Offence	$ Personal loss per average offence
Robbery	284
Burglary	390
Auto theft	1,017
Grand theft	239
Petty theft	26
Homicide	93,000
Aggravated assault	200
Forcible rape	200

10.410 The Table shows the values Shoup and Mehay attach to different offences. The financial loss from robbery is calculated as the average of all robberies which took place in the state of California within a specified period. The same holds good for the components, financial loss and damage, for all other offences. Where offences involve loss of life or injury, road accident figures are added.

10.411 A general criticism of the Shoup–Mehay valuation is that thefts are valued as the amount stolen, whereas we have tried to justify the view that the true social loss is up to twice the amount stolen. But the major drawback of the Shoup–Mehay approach is its total neglect of two important elements in victims' losses from crime:

(a) pain and suffering

(b) feelings of outrage at violation of person or property. These omissions no doubt go some way to explain the curious relativities embodied in the Shoup–Mehay table. To take but an extreme example, the implication is that society would rather prevent one car theft (value $1,017) than five rapes (value $1,000).

10.412 There are two ways in which the missing elements could be provided:

(i) by a survey of potential victims

(ii) by postulated values promulgated by the decision-maker.

The former may be regarded as the more remote of these alternatives. Possibly use could be made of the hypothetical choice method. Give the 'consumer' a hypothetical increase or decrease in his budget and widen his choice set to include a range of probabilities of becoming a victim, since this is a variable the police aim to reduce. Until this programme can be carried out, however, we will probably have to make do with values postulated by a decision-maker.

10.5 The Lancaster system

10.51 We have seen that because the various agencies in the criminal justice system together produce the good results, it is necessary to add downstream costs to police costs to derive the total cost of the good result. It will not do simply to maximize the value of output per £ of police expenditure. We also saw that great care was necessary in computing these costs to ensure that true social costs were brought to light and not merely public spending. We then considered the problems of valuing the good results in money terms and saw that while more work needs to be done in this area, some rules of thumb had merit.

10.52 Now we will consider an important study of police efficiency, in fact, the most comprehensive investigation of its kind in the UK, undertaken by the University of Lancaster Operations Research Department. It will be plain that the approach they adopt by no means conforms with the precepts we have put forward above. The point of difference being obvious, we will not on the whole draw attention to them. Attention will, however, be drawn to the important consequences of some seemingly innocuous assumptions the investigators make in the interests of tractability. Nonetheless, we cite the Lancaster work for its solid merits, for it marks an important step on the road to the ideal.

10.53 The prime objective of the study was to throw light on the most effective deployment of existing police resources in the Lancaster Division. Three main problems had to be faced:

(a) enumeration and valuation of the output of the division.

(b) measuring the productivity of various police activities and arrangements in terms of this output.

(c) identifying the most efficient mix of activities and deployment.

(a) VALUATION PROBLEMS

10.54 The investigators at once recognized that the output of a police force is very heterogenous. But even before this heterogeneity is faced it is necessary to establish what will be counted as a good result and therefore form part of the output of the system. Some good results are immediately and easily identified, e.g. the deterrence of crime, the detection and apprehension of offenders. Also, however, the police are expected to contribute to the prevention of accidents and congestion, and these are ends which can be promoted in ways other than by apprehension and detections of offenders. This involves the police in activities that may be unconnected with offences, such as sorting out traffic jams, warning oncoming motorists of unexpected road hazards. The recovery and restoration to rightful owners of stolen goods are also regarded as good results. Finally, there are certain other achievements which could be classed as giving assistance to members of the community which are totally unconnected with any offence, e.g. tracing missing persons, assisting ill, senile or deficient persons, resolving domestic disputes.

10.55 Even within the category of good results a distinction is drawn betwen end and non-end results. Prevention of crime is a good thing in itself in that it avoids harm for someone. Detection and apprehension of criminals, however, are non-end results, only good inasfar as they promote future end results such as prevented crimes. In determining the direction of police effort between prevention and detection, detections would have to be weighted by their prevention value. If the prevention value of a detection were very low, if, that is, the criminal justice system were totally ineffective in changing the subsequent careers of convicted offenders, it would not be worth devoting great effort to detection but better to spend a lot of time on preventive patrol. If on the other hand the detection, apprehension and process through the criminal justice system of offenders did bring about a great reduction in future crimes then clearly detection and apprehension would be the proper goals of the main thrust of effort. However, in the value judgement survey there is little point in asking respondents to score detections rather than preventions unless they have knowledge of the effectiveness of the whole CJS in reducing future crime, knowledge, that is, of the prevention value of a detection. In the value judgement survey, therefore, respondents were asked only to score good *end* results.

10.56 The next problem is who is to do the scoring? The Lancaster investigators chose a group of senior police officers, ranked sergeant and above. It is clear, however, that this choice is merely a matter of convenience since it was easy to secure the cooperation of the police and the investigators hoped that the scores of these respondents would be those of society as a whole.

10.57 The method was to present respondents with a set of crimes to score in terms of some offence arbitrarily chosen as the standard of reference, viz. the simple larceny of £10, which was given the value 1. All other results were to be rated as the number of larcenies of £10 which would be worth incurring to achieve the result in question. It proved rather difficult to bring respondents to think of results in this way, but we will not here go into the fascinating story of the difficulties the investigators met nor how they overcame them. Suffice it to say that a scale was produced which the investigators were satisfied was adequate for their experimental objectives.

10.58 Out of the infinity of gradations and combinations of criminal acts and other bad outcomes of human activity 75 separate incidents are given preventive value in the index. A selection is presented in the table on page 128.

10.59 The investigators express concern at the way respondents have scored money losses, scores rising markedly less than in proportion to the amount stolen. Take simple larceny as a case in point. The inference is that the scorers would prefer to prevent larceny of £7 if taken in £1 lots rather than larceny of £1,000 taken at one fell swoop. The investigators plainly feel that scorings proportional, or more nearly proportional, to money loss is in some sense correct. They therefore speculate as to the reasons for the discrepancy. The reason might be that the value of property stolen is fortuitous and what is important is the fact of stealing it. The investigators would not accept this as a good reason as they feel that the amount of harm

	Prevention Value
Indictable offences	
Simple Larceny, £1	0·63
,, £10 (standard of reference)	1·0
,, £100	1·8
,, £1000	3·7
Larceny of pedal cycle, £10	0·24
,, from shops, stalls, £10	0·77
,, in dwelling house, £10	8·00
,, of car, £100	1·6
Shopbreaking, £1	1·8
,, £10	2·8
,, £100	3·6
,, £1000	6·8
Housebreaking, £10	13
Unarmed Robbery, slight injury, £10	11
Armed Robbery, slight injury, £10	25
Armed Robbery, serious injury, £10	32
Rape, slight injury	36
Rape, serious injury	47
Felonious wounding, serious injury	22
Murder	210
Prevention of non-indictable and traffic offences	
Drunkenness, simple	0·48
Breach of peace	0·9
Assault on constable	5·0
Parking and obstruction	0·1
Speeding	0·23
Careless driving	0·57
Driving under influence	10·0
Other achievements	
Prevent traffic congestion,	
1000 people × 10 mins	0·25
Prevent traffic accident, £10	0·32
Recover stolen property, £10	0·51
Resolve domestic dispute	0·05
Rectify insecure premises	0·1
Assist ill, senile or deficient person	0·25
Trace missing person	0·39

done is directly related to the amount stolen, however uncertain that is from the point of view of the larcenist. Respondents might, however, harbour the notion that the large amounts are stolen from victims well able to bear them, e.g. firms and well-to-do individuals, and that the social valuation of money or property lost by the well-to-do is lower than the same value of loss for less prosperous people. The investigators feel this would be an acceptable explanation for the pattern of scores as it incorporates a distributional value judgement which is not present in cost-benefit analysis and which, moreover, they feel to be a lack in it.

10.510 In applying the index a certain amount of simplification was found necessary. Since the productivity of public preventive activity can only be measured in terms of broad classifications such as indictable, non-indictable etc., average scores for these groups had to be produced. This was done by weighting the prevention values of the main value judgement index by the number of reported incidents of each type.

10.511 When it comes to the measurement of the preventive worth of a detection additional problems arise. Certain of the respondents were asked to rate detections as well as preventions, having been strictly enjoined to set down how many preventions they thought would result from a detection. As the figures obtained lay within the narrow range 1·02 to 1·10, the investigators felt that no confidence could be placed in the results, the respondents plainly having misunderstood what was required of them. A different approach was therefore adopted. For indictable offences the detection value was taken to be (a) proportional to the preventive value on the assumption that those not caught for an offence are likely to repeat it (b) inversely proportional to the *detection rate* since the lower the detection rate the more offences of that type the offender is likely to have committed by the time he is actually apprehended. A similar approach was used for other classes of incident.

10.512 The measure of effectiveness actually used in the experiment was:

20 (no. of indictables prevented)$+20k_1$ (no. of indictables detected)

$+5$ (no. of non-indictables prevented)$+5k_2$ (no. of non-indictables detected)

$+10$ (no. of accidents prevented)$+2k_3$ (no. of traffic offences detected)

$+10$ (no. of 000s of man-hours of congestion prevented)

$+1k_4$ (no. of emergencies handled).

It should be noted that 10 units of effectiveness correspond to the value of preventing a typical larceny (1.66 points on the value judgement index). The k's are preventive values of detection. It is plain that what we have now is a rather crude output index since good results are classed very broadly and prevention values so uncertain as to dictate recourse to sensitivity analysis in evaluating the outputs of alternative uses of police resources.

(b) PRODUCTIVITY OF RESOURCES

10.513 In most applications of cost-effectiveness analysis, the analysts are not burdened with the task of throwing light on the production function of resources in promoting the end result. In Chapter Seven where we discussed cost-benefit analysis, we referred to Blumstein's cost-effectiveness analysis of ways of reducing delay in response to police emergency calls. There the production function was a datum. In the Lancaster study, however, the task of bringing the production function to light was a crucial and integral part of the whole project. Moreover, we contend that certain of the assumptions which the investigators made in the absence of hard data have an important bearing on the results likely to be obtained. We are therefore forced to say something on this topic, although in most cost-effectiveness analysis it would not require attention.

10.514 Patrol activity results are classified as either 'marginal' or 'non-marginal'. A 'non-marginal' result is achieved by any pattern of patrol deployment provided that some patrol is actually available. Since a certain minimum level of readiness is adopted as a constraint in the maximization exercise we will say no more about it. However, 'marginal' results depend for their achievement on the level of the operation by which they are expected to be achieved. These are of three kinds:

(i) prevention results, the offences which do not take place because of police patrol,

(ii) response-time results, the essence of which is that a patrol reacts to an emergency call quickly enough to apprehend the offender on the spot,

(iii) discoveries, where the police actually come across an incident in progress.

On these points, the evidence available is as follows:

(i) The only evidence available, for foot patrols in the pre-car era, suggested that patrol strengths beyond one man per standard beat were unsuccessful in preventing additional offences. The investigators therefore determined the car patrol equivalent of one man per standard beat and assumed that beyond this level marginal product was nil.

(ii) Given the spatial distribution of offences and of cars, it is possible to work out the probability of achieving a response-time result for a given deployment and number of cars. From the way the formula is constructed it is apparent that the marginal productivity of cars in this use declines as their numbers increase.

(iii) The discoveries model is *based* on the assumption of constant marginal productivity. The discoveries made depend on the time of day and the district of the division. But these factors simply act as constants of proportionality: double the number of cars and you double the number of discoveries. That is the postulate.

(c) OPTIMAL DEPLOYMENT OF RESOURCES

10.515 When it comes to the question of the optimal deployment of resources a few salient facts about the index and the production functions appear to guarantee what the result is going to be. Take the index first. Here the investigators were punctilious in their desire to have the respondents' marginal values (in terms of index points) of the results. But there is no provision for the marginal value of any result to decline relative to other results if it is abundantly achieved relative to them. It is still apparently worth 210 larcenies of £1 to prevent a murder whether there is much murder relative to larceny or vice versa. Moreover, we have just drawn attention to a linear marginal productivity schedule in one aspect of the production function. We would therefore predict that to maximize the value of the index it would eventually be worth deploying patrols to discover the type of incident with respect to which the productivity of patrols is greatest. That is we would not get a mix of patrols doing different things, we would get them all doing one thing. We would have a situation like that shown on page 132.

The marginal value product of patrol units deployed in discovery (marginal product x value of offence) would be as depicted in the diagram. The MV Prod of units in one use lies either wholly above or wholly below the MV Prod of units in other uses. Therefore to maximize the index we wouldn't distribute units around types of result, we would concentrate them where their MV Prod was greatest, i.e. use z. Now, *either* of two factors would cause the MV Prod schedule to slope down: (i) the marginal product in terms of the type of result sloped down (ii) the marginal value of the result sloped down as the level at which it was being achieved rose. But, apparently without giving the matter much thought, the investigators have not allowed

Points

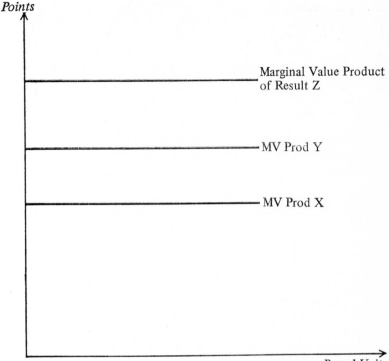

Marginal Value Product
of Result Z

MV Prod Y

MV Prod X

Patrol Units

the possibility of either. Even if for other 'marginal' results the
marginal product schedule is declining so that their MV prods are,
to start with at any rate, above the MV Prod of discovering incident
z, their very decline ensures that eventually resources will be concentrated on discovering z. Supposing that the marginal value
productivities of units in achieving results through rapid response,
prevention and discovery are like the diagrams on the opposite page.
The overall deployment of a given number of patrol units (e.g. OA)
would seek to achieve the highest marginal value product (solid line)
(see diagram on page 134). Moreover if patrol units are to be increased in number to OB, plainly all would go on discovery of z.

10.516 This is not just a remote possibility: this is the result
actually achieved on the first optimizing run of the model. Apart
from some town centre patrols deployed to meet the readiness constraint, all other units are put to traffic patrol. The results therefore
perpetuate the linearities of the assumptions, thereby illustrating the

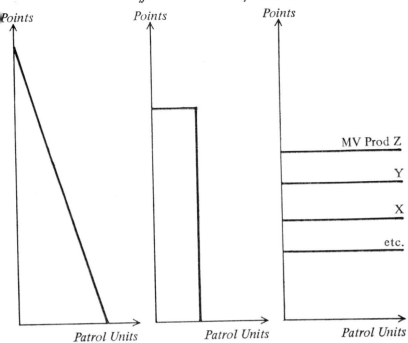

Response Results   Preventive Patrol   Discovery

extreme outcomes of apparently innocuous assumptions. The investigators get round this problem by postulating that the MV of
traffic results falls to nothing after a certain level of achievement,
actually chosen to be that of the year previous to the study. This is
of course a totally arbitrary procedure.

WHAT PRICE A SERIOUSNESS POINT?

10.517 In general we may ask if this study could be made into a
cost-benefit analysis. The cost of inputs actually is carefully calculated by the investigators; the output, however, is denominated in
seriousness points. There are two ways in which the two quantities
can be married. Firstly, a seriousness point implicitly has a value
already—the amount of money it is thought to be worth spending
to achieve a point at the margin. This could be elucidated by maxi-
mizing the value of the index for a slightly altered input constraint.
How many points would be gained or lost if one patrol unit, costing
£x, is added to or subtracted from the stock of inputs? The change

Points

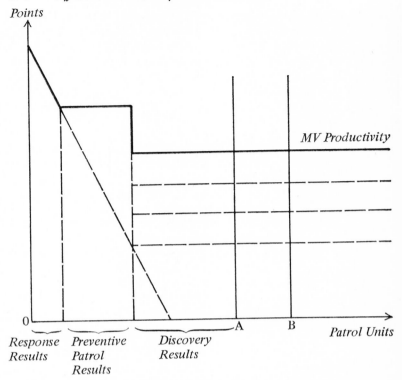

in the maximum value of points divided by £x gives the number of points per £. This may be looked upon as unsatisfactory since the value of the output emerges as an outcome of the optimization exercise, not as an input to it. A second method is to explore points of contact between scores for accident prevention on the Lancaster scale and the money values placed on the same incidents by the Department of the Environment in assessing the worthwhileness of safety factors in road investment. This turns out to be rather inconclusive since the ratios between incidents differ in the two systems. Mention has already been made of the non-proportionality of Lancaster scores with time lost through congestion. Again the two systems exhibit different ratios. Attempts to put a money value on a seriousness point have therefore proved somewhat inconclusive.

EXTERNALITIES

10.518 It can fairly be counted against the Lancaster study that it ignores important externalities. The externalities of police activities are not imposed upon private individuals or firms but upon other public agencies. This point has particular relevance to the issue of preventions versus detections. The investigators rightly try to estimate the greater non-police costs associated with a detection. Recall that while a prevention imposes no extra cost on the agencies downstream of the police—the courts and prison/probation service—a detection does. So when the investigators assume that a detection is worth k preventions they are taking into account the benefits produced by the downstream agencies but not taking into account their costs. Strictly speaking as we have said before, those responsible for deploying police resources should maximize the value of the index with respect not only to the cost of a given level of police resources but to the costs of the *whole* criminal justice system. And while it is reasonable to suppose that the stock of resources available for a police division is fixed, the same assumption cannot be made about the courts and prisons since for them some categories of cost do vary with the volume of custom presented to them. We are forced back therefore to consider a problem where the input and output of the system are both variable and therefore to seek an optimum at which the marginal value of the output is equal to the marginal cost of the input, a task to which the Lancaster framework is not well-suited.

10.6 Distributional matters

10.61 Finally, it should be noted that the Lancaster approach to the valuation of output does not itself lead directly to consideration of distributional questions. Yet there are few places in which distributional questions bob up more obstinately than in the field of crime control. Two distinct problems can be identified:

(i) the geographical distribution of police protection,
(ii) the implications for the overall distribution of wealth and income of the pattern of gains and losses through crime.

We take these points in turn:

(i) This is nothing but the general problem of equity versus efficiency in a particular guise: should the police authorities deploy the resources at their disposal so as to minimize the amount of crime in the area of their jurisdiction, even if this means that some areas will be left with higher crime rates than others? Minimization of the total number of crimes, or, preferably, the value of some crime index, is identified with the promotion of efficiency, while equalization of the incidence of crime per head would be the policy that

K

springs most readily to mind if equity were the foremost consideration. One way out of the dilemma is to pay compensation to the
victims of crime: if police resources were then deployed so as to
minimize the value of some crime index, the undesirable consequences for equity could be eliminated by compensation. But if
no such solution can be operated, the dilemma is a real problem of
which the decision-maker should be aware.

(ii) It has been suggested that less weight should be attached to
the losses of victims than to the gains of offenders because (or so it is
alleged) the latter are generally poorer than the former. Specifically,
it has been suggested that the losses of victims should be reduced
(notionally, for planning purposes only) by the marginal rate of tax
to which their income is subject. If the object is to adjust for income
distribution this does not seem to be the correct procedure since
adjustment has already been made: unless the victim happens to
be a skilful tax-dodger, a thief snatching his wallet plunders him of
after-tax income. Since the welfare significance of everyone's *after-
tax* £'s is the same the proposed weighting seems wrong. Indeed the
argument appears to apply the other way round. Since offenders'
gains are not subject to tax in the same way as legitimate income,
the social valuation of illicit income ought to be reduced by the
marginal tax rate that would have applied had the income been
legitimate.

10.62 A variant of the previous argument is that society ought not
to be unduly concerned at shoplifting on the grounds that shoplifters
are poorer than shopowners. The main difference between this
variant and the main argument is the dubious assumption about
who bears the loss. Shopowners are likely to try to recoup losses by
raising prices so as to earn as much after losses have been allowed
for as they could in areas where losses are low. In that case honest
shoppers are paying for the gains of dishonest shoppers and the
allegation that shoplifting redistributes income from rich to poor
cannot be sustained.

10.63 This airing of the distributional issue has been brief but
will it is hoped alert the reader to other instances. The great thing is
not to allow these issues to go by default.

Additional Reading

This is perhaps the most difficult chapter on which to offer guidance.
Most of the work on the economics of crime and crime control
involves sophisticated concepts and techniques rather beyond the
general reader—even when he has become less general by having

read this book. However, on the question of valuing prevented crimes, the following may be of interest:

T. Sellin and M. E. Wolfgang, *The Measurement of Delinquency*, John Wiley & Sons Inc., New York, 1964.

D. R. Kaye and V. Watts, 'The Development of Improved Measures of the Success of the CID and their Possible Use', Discussion Paper presented at a Royal Economic Society Conference on Decision Analysis, Lancaster, 1973.

D. C. Shoup, 'Cost Effectiveness of Traffic Law Enforcement', *Journal of Transport Economics and Policy*, Vol. VII, No. 1, 1973.

As a complement to Shoup the following may also be of interest:

L. C. Thurow, and C. Rapporport, 'Law Enforcement and Cost-Benefit Analysis', *Public Finance*, Vol. 24, No. 1, 1969.

An interesting issue is raised in L. C. Thurow, 'Equity versus Efficiency in Law Enforcement', *Public Policy*, No. 4, 1970.

CHAPTER ELEVEN

Epilogue

11.1 Introduction

11.11 By now the reader will have discerned a central vein of common material and ideas running through this book from beginning to end. We have been concerned throughout with priorities, with alternative modes of provision of service, and with costs, and with an evaluative framework which brings these key elements together in a systematic and comparable manner.

11.2 Priorities

11.21 The problem of priorities arises because we cannot do everything we would like to do, and because we reject simple market mechanisms such as financial profitability as adequate tests for determining what the priorities should be. Yet priorities are still a matter of relative valuation, and if these relative valuations are not to come through profitability tests, where are they to come from?

11.22 There are basically three answers, which are not mutually exclusive. The first is that they should come directly from the clients, or potential clients, for the services. The second is that they should come from those who make the sacrifices in order that the services shall be provided. The third is that they shall come from some detached third parties, with special expertise or legitimate authority to 'arbitrate' between the (usually) conflicting interests of the first two groups.

11.23 It will be obvious that this tidy three-way split is rather confused in practice because many of the readers of this book will play all three roles at one time or another, and most people in the community at large will play the first two. Nevertheless, it is useful to see what kind of information relevant to priorities each group might see as relevant, and how it would get processed within our framework.

11.24 The first group were the beneficiaries themselves, and the market mechanism would have enabled them to express their priorities through bidding for services (i.e. willingness and ability to pay), which in turn means that to accept that mode for expressing priorities we would need to believe

(1) that individuals are the best judges of their own welfare

(2) that they have adequate information on which to base a choice

(3) that the distribution of bidding power (money, time, etc.) is appropriate.

11.25 If (3) is rejected, but (1) and (2) accepted, then it is still possible to get priority evaluation simulated in market type situations where potential access is made 'appropriate' (e.g. by the distribution of vouchers, ration coupons, etc.). Out of this a different 'price-structure' will emerge (i.e. in terms of voucher or coupon prices) from the money-price structure. In some situations money prices are rejected entirely, and no vouchers or substitute 'money' offered, so the 'purchasing power' becomes a time-or-energy 'price' (i.e. willingness or ability to wait in line for service, or persistence in repeatedly demanding service), which raises the same issue again as to whether this is an appropriate 'distributional' basis for access. All this 'price' information could be processed, (if acceptable as a statement of the relative priorities as seen by well-informed clients who are the best judges of their own welfare) in the way in which market-price information is processed, taking high valued units of service first, ranking them in descending order of value, and continuing until we reach the unit where marginal value just equals its marginal cost.

11.26 If, however, we reject either (1) or (2), we could not allow clients' own valuations to be decisive, whatever our attitude to (3). We might still, however, wish to know what the clients' valuations were, but we would then wish to modify them, *either* in the light of information we have which they do not have,* *or* because we regard them as competent to make such evaluations in certain areas for which we are responsible, if not in others (e.g. the views of criminals may be regarded irrelevant to the issue of whether or not they

---

* Which raises an issue not discussed here, namely, *why* they do not have it.

should be imprisoned, but not as to the nature of any industrial rehabilitation service which might be offered to them).

11.27 This brings us to the second group of possible priority setters, those footing the bill. 'He who pays the piper calls the tune' is a time-honoured principle, not viewed with universal favour, but it certainly reflects a common stance on the subject of priority-setting. But whatever its merits, it runs into the same difficulties as we have already noted, i.e. how are such priorities to be articulated in practice? At one extreme we could have a 'market' syndrome ... a subscription list for each particular type of service provision, so that we get lots of provision of services which 'attract' money, and not much of those which don't. This clearly raises questions (1), (2) and (3) again, this time with respect to donors, rather than recipients, and we could again go through the same arguments and reach the same conclusions, *mutatis mutandis*.

11.28 It is, therefore, not surprising that a characteristic response has been to rely on the third group, the 'arbitrators'—be they politicians, administrators, experts, or whatever—to adjudicate on priorities, within varying mechanisms and degrees of explicitness, and varying degrees (and mechanisms) of public accountability. It has been to this group that most of this book has been addressed, because they are frequently placed in the most invidious and confusing position, i.e. told to get on with the job of priority setting which beneficiaries and cost bearers cannot readily do for themselves, yet to remain responsive (in unstated proportions) to the (differing) and inarticulate wishes of these two groups.

11.29 As we said at the outset, we have not presumed to advise on how this minefield is to be negotiated, but we have tried to indicate what information about priorities could be relevant, how it might be processed, and what some of the pitfalls are. Our basic theme has been that priority setting is essentially a matter of measuring benefits at the margin, whether the *values* that are used in that process come from clients, taxpayers, or the policy makers themselves (or, indeed, some amalgam of all three).

11.3 Alternatives

11.31 The perception of alternatives is a logical prerequisite for the exercise of choice, and the exercise of choice is both the essence and the substance (as opposed to the rhetoric) of policy-making in the social services. Thus the manner in which alternatives are formulated in the decision-making process is critical to the pursuit of efficiency in the social services.

11.32 It is widely believed that there is little that analysis (economic or otherwise) can do to widen the room for manoeuvre within a social service. If one sees analysis as restricted to the evaluation of a predetermined set of alternatives (and especially if these alternatives boil down to X or nothing!) then its scope and value will certainly be severely curtailed. But it would be foolish and short-sighted to see its role in this way.

11.33 In the first place the analysis of a proposed course of action will frequently lead the analyst to question the purpose of providing those clients with that service in that place at that time in that manner with those inputs. He will do so not out of sheer bloody-mindedness, but because he needs the answers to understand and formulate the problem for analysis. In the process of educating himself, the analyst may well ask, why do you do it so rather than some other way. It may turn out that there is no good reason, prima facie, for not doing it this other way, and it may well be that the study gets extended to include that option. Thus the process of analysis may itself throw up imaginative new ideas for how a service might be run. This is not to say that these new options will necessarily survive further critical scrutiny within the subsequent analysis, of course, but it does indicate that analysis need not (and should not) be seen as a passive, uncreative, activity. It should also be added that it is not only the analyst who may be stimulated in this way during the exploratory analytical dialogue, for the people running the service are equally 'vulnerable' to this serendipitous process, and may equally well be sparked off into new perceptions of what might be done.

11.34 At a second, and broader level, lies the power of analysis to facilitate sweeping generalizations. I realize that this is also not universally regarded as an asset, indeed by some it is the first sign that things are going off the rails. But there are often very interesting insights to be obtained by seeking out and exploring apparently comparable situations in widely different contexts. For instance, the issue of inpatient, outpatient and intensive domiciliary care, which by virtue of the terminology, will immediately be recognized as a major policy problem in the field of health and welfare services, has strong analogues in the field of education, and even stronger ones in the field of crime control. The notion of 'treatment' spans all three, as does the professionalization of treatment providers, the problems of measuring and evaluating effectiveness, and the sizeable public

142   *Epilogue*

investment, and consequent issues of central versus local control, etc. It is an interesting and not entirely idle field for speculation as to whether our health and welfare services should be run more like education services or our 'corrective' services, or vice versa! On a narrower front, one might consider whether the solutions to particular problems adopted in one might not also be worth considering, with appropriate adaptation, for another. Certainly the evidence on the strong influence of socio-economic background on the problems and achievements of all three services suggests more than a casual linkage between them.

11.4 Costs

11.41 Our basic theme here has been that the notion of costs transcends money expenditures, and will frequently be poorly represented thereby. Since 'cost' means 'sacrifice', whenever anyone asks 'what will it cost?' one should immediately translate that question into 'what must be sacrificed?' If costs are reformulated and calculated in that way, it is hard to see why anyone would resist a policy of cost-minimization (at a constant level of effectiveness) since it simply means the avoidance of unnecessary sacrifices.

11.42 We have, however, indicated that it is not at all simple to go beyond accounting notions of cost, so this is not a prescription that is costlessly made up, and in the immediate future much will depend on the perspicacity of the people running social services to identify from experience the areas where the greatest and most dangerous discrepancies are likely to arise between the notions of cost which actually inform the decisions that are taken, and the notions of cost which ought to do so, and then to set in train some process which will put things right.

11.43 Our experience has indicated that the three most common weaknesses in this field are

(a) counting only the items that fall on the agency's own budget;

(b) failing to distinguish average and marginal costs; and

(c) not knowing how to take proper account of the differential timing of alternative cost streams.

A fourth problem, closely associated with (b), is the failure to realize that resources which are already irretrievably committed can be left out of analysis of any prospective decision, except in so far as they affect the deployment of further resources. This is because the sacrifice has been made, and will remain whatever is done next.

11.5 *Envoi*

11.51 Our object has been to demonstrate that the notion of priorities, part of the common parlance of policy making and decision taking in the social services, can be given useful operational content and processed within the framework of micro-economics as a schedule of marginal valuations of 'outputs' from social services, where the notion of 'output' has lost all connotations of tangibility or marketability. When this is put together with a schedule of marginal costs, which also go much wider than mere money outlays, we have the classic micro-economic framework of choice, perfectly simulated, so that we are able to use all of its analytical insights, without having to accept the commercial and profit-seeking notions which underlie its applications to the business situation.

11.52 This should not really be surprising, nor viewed as an insight, nor even as a despicable sleight-of-hand, because economics is fundamentally about resource-allocation, and it is only by historical accident that it has concentrated so much on money as a resource, and on market systems of allocation, and on markets dominated by profit-seeking behaviour. Economists have long recognized that even to understand how markets work as *real* resource-allocating mechanisms we need to peer behind 'the veil of money' into the deployment of human skills, capital equipment, raw materials, buildings, land, etc. Economists have also been taking increasing interest in non-market mechanisms for allocating resources, but their work has not yet made a very deep impact on the teaching of the subject at introductory level, beyond which most people do not go. We are trying to short-circuit that process by leaping in where the more cautious and scholarly of our colleagues still fear to tread.

11.53 We are conscious of two opposing dangers which we have courted in doing so. The first is that our professional colleagues in economics will accuse us of glib oversimplification, i.e. skating on thin ice at times in order to get quickly to the main point. To this we must plead guilty, just as must any honest exposition of elementary principles. Our only defence is that we have striven hard to ensure that the things we have excluded are less important than the things we have included, given the interests of our readership.

11.54 The second danger is that our readers in other walks of life will accuse us of propogating a counsel of perfection, in advocating the use of economists' tools in a context in which they are severely constrained by intense political pressure, bureaucratic inertia, lack of data, lack of analytical staff, and a desperate air of impending breakdown which totally absorbs their energies and attention. Well, it would be a pity to leave things with a counsel of perfection matched by a counsel of despair, so let us see if we can end on a more constructive, yet realistic, note.

11.55 There will frequently be opportunities for analytical work in an organization, even when hard-pressed, provided those running it see its value. It is a matter of priorities. Current problems versus future problems. It may be that current crises are partly due to too little analysis in the past, and if so the message for the future is obvious, if ever the organization is to get out of a rather vicious spiral. One of our objectives has been to enable readers to spot such opportunities more effectively.

11.56 But the social services are of such widespread interest to the community at large, that one should not think that all analytical work need originate, or be conducted by, those services themselves, though their cooperation will often be necessary, and occasionally essential. Where the role of the policy-maker or decision-maker in the social services is absolutely essential, however, is in appraising and absorbing the results of analytical studies, irrespective of who did them, or how and where they were done. Thus our other main objective has been to facilitate this important function, which we could round off, in a down-to-earth way, by offering the following checklist of questions* for the hard-pressed reader to prop up on his or her desk as a text for the day! It should be consulted whenever a report lands on your desk offering you studied advice on how to improve the efficiency of any social service (we assume that you would reject *un*studied advice out of hand anyway!)

 (1) What precisely is the question which the study was trying to answer?
 (2) What is the question that it has actually answered?
 (3) What are the assumed objectives of the activity studied?
 (4) By what measures are these represented?
 (5) How are they weighted?
 (6) Do they enable us to tell whether the objectives are being attained?
 (7) What range of options was considered?
 (8) What other options might there have been?
 (9) Were they rejected, or not considered, for good reasons?

* Originally published in Alan Williams, 'The Cost-Benefit Approach', *British Medical Bulletin* (1974) Vol. 30, No. 3, pp. 252–6.

(10) Would their inclusion have been likely to change the results?

(11) Is anyone likely to be affected who has not been considered in the analysis?

(12) If so, why are they excluded?

(13) Does the notion of cost go wider or deeper than the expenditure of the agency concerned?

(14) If not, is it clear that these expenditures cover all the resources used and accurately represent their value if released for other uses?

(15) If so, is the line drawn so as to include all potential beneficiaries and losers, and are resources costed at their value in their best alternative use?

(16) Is the differential timing of the items in the streams of benefits and costs suitably taken care of (e.g. by discounting, and, if so, at what rate)?

(17) Where there is uncertainty, or there are known margins of error, is it made clear how sensitive the outcome is to these elements?

(18) Are the results, on balance, good enough for the job in hand?

(19) Has anyone else done better?

The last two questions are our defence against the accusations of purveying a counsel of perfection. We recognize that decisions do have to be made, and will continue to be made, on the basis of imperfect knowledge. But we are anxious to ensure that we know how little we know when we do what we have to do.

Glossary

Consumers' surplus from a set of units of a good is their total valuation of these units (sum of their marginal valuations) less what they have to pay for them.

Cost-Benefit Analysis (CBA) is a method for assessing the desirability of some prospective change. It involves the enumeration and valuation in money terms of all relevant costs and benefits, no matter when they occur or to whom they accrue.

Cost-Effectiveness Analysis (CEA) is the procedure of identifying the least-cost means of achieving a given objective.

Discounting is a procedure whereby a stream of costs or benefits incurred or accruing at different points in time is expressed as an equivalent sum of money at a single point in time, normally the present. This single sum is in the latter case referred to as the *Present Value*. The rate of exchange between sums of money accruing or occurring at different points in time is known as the discount rate.

Economies of Scale are said to be present when cost per unit is less at a high level of output than at a low level.

Marginal Cost (MC) is the extra cost of producing an extra unit of output, given some particular level of output (e.g. 0, 10, 12 units).

Marginal Product of an input is the extra output that would be produced by adding an extra unit of the input to some pre-existing set of inputs.

Marginal Rate of Time Preference is the rate at which an individual is prepared to transfer an extra £ between time periods, given a particular endowment of money or income in the two periods.

A Marginal Valuation Schedule or Curve plots marginal values over a range of quantities of a good.

Marginal Value (MV) is the value a consumer places on an extra unit of a good, given that he consumes a particular quantity already.

Opportunity Cost is the value of what is given up by doing one thing rather than another.

Present Value. See Discounting.

Rate of Discount is another term for the rate of interest.

Shadow Price is a price attached to a resource for planning purposes to reflect true value in a case where actual price fails to do so, e.g. if there is a 'shortage' of nurses a shadow wage higher than the actual wage should be used when considering substitutions with other inputs, the aim being to represent the true scarcity of nurses.

Index

This book is intended to help the large number of people in the social services responsible for decisions committing resources which are in short supply, be these money, materials or manpower.

The authors analyse the notion of 'efficiency' to discover its relevance to the social services. Their object is to give readers a keen appreciation of the strengths and weaknesses of the different approaches to 'efficiency' implicit in reports and recommendations to which they may be exposed. Basic microeconomic principles are shown to be just as relevant in the non-commercial environment of the social services as they are in the field of business.

The exposition, though systematic, is not at all technical, and is aimed at social service professionals and students, social administrators, lay members of management bodies, policy makers and the ordinary citizen who wishes to see more clearly through the rhetorical fog which often obscures the subject. No prior knowledge of economics, mathematics or statistics is assumed; merely an intelligent awareness of some key issues in practical social policy, and sufficient interest to follow a logical argument through to its conclusions.

The opening chapters are devoted to concrete situations which pose down-to-earth problems; for each one, solutions are offered and the principles on which those solutions are based are examined. The later chapters survey actual cases where such principles have been applied.

Alan Williams is a Professor in the Department of Economics at the University of York. He is the author of numerous publications on government budgeting and cost-benefit analysis.
Robert Anderson is a Research Fellow of the Institute of Social and Economic Research at the University of York. He has published on the economics of recreation and of crime.

Basil Blackwell & Martin Robertson

Also in this series:

Social Policy
A survey of recent developments
Edited by Michael H. Cooper

Provision for the Disabled
Eda Topliss

The Child's Generation
Jean Packman

Forthcoming:

Penal Policy
A. E. Bottoms

Capitalism and Social Welfare
A comparative study
Roger Lawson

Of Related Interest:

Social and Economic Administration
published three times a year by Basil Blackwell for the University of Exeter
Editor: R. A. B. Leaper

Cover design by Nicholas Rous